View to the future

# View to the future Graphic design to-day and to-morrow

This publication is made possible through the support
of the Ministry of Education Culture and Science and by
the Production fund Jan van Eyck Akademie with
contributions from the Province of Limburg, the
Municipality of Maastricht and Drukkerij Lecturis bv,
Eindhoven.

ISBN 90-6617-184-7 (De Balie)

Paul Hefting
View to the Future

The Jan van Eyck Akademie is a post-academic institute and it
is clear that at such a place thought goes into what is
officially called 'professional practice'. The project View to
the Future is an example of this. But the initiators were not
concerned only with the future practice of the graphic design
profession, but also with its background, its history and the
outlook with which the profession can, and perhaps should be
pursued. An inventory of the recent past would perhaps provide
pointers for the future. And then there are the technical
developments in the printing world. These go so fast and are so
spectacular that it is hard to imagine what position a graphic
designer should take in relation to them. But these
developments, however fast, have also been happening in the
recent past and in that sense too it was interesting to ask
some prominent Dutch designers to share their experiences and
opinions about the profession and its future.

At the end of 1995 eight participants of the Jan van Eyck
Akademie and eight designers from several generations embarked
upon the project which now, over a year and a half later, has
resulted in the publication View to the Future, in which eight
participants have recorded their experiences and views on the
recent past, the present and the future of graphic design. The
project has been co-ordinated by Karel Martens of the Jan van
Eyck Akademie, and Paul Hefting, art historian. The British
critic Robin Kinross wrote for the publication a personal
view on the design profession.

There are three departments at the Jan van Eyck Akademie:
fine art, design and theory. Much value is given to the latter,
because participants are expected not only to have or to
receive the necessary intellectual baggage for the future but
also, so to speak, to 'arm' themselves against the
intellectual decay and uncritical acceptance of modern
culture. This is particularly complicated in the field of
design because there is always a third party involved; the
commissioning client. This means that instead of autonomy we
have to speak of a form of 'service provision', in which the
end result has to come about in as good and fruitful a
negotiation as possible. The big question is to what extent the
designer has to be subservient to the client or to be critical
so as possibly to change the client's mind and bring him to a

5

different formulation of the assignment. As a designer one can
be 'autonomous' and take a critical stance, independent of any
commission - and in education this may well be the approach to
theory that is needed - in practice it has to be seen how
tenable such a stance is. And are we talking then about form or
content? Is it about a concern with a form of idealism, an
involvement in society, or about a strictly formal,
professional approach? Criticism for the sake of it does not
provide a solution in any case. At the very least this is a
dilemma which everyone has to solve for himself in his own way
in a world geared towards a market economy, a world which does
not look like becoming simpler. This is why a dialogue between
designers and those who commission them could be a logical next
step from this initial investigation of the future, not least
to test the possibilities for a critical attitude with respect
to theory and practice.

    View to the Future was in the first place an educational
project - thinking about the profession and its future and
going on to formulate these thoughts. For a designer this
formulating and communicating of ideas is part of his
profession, in the same way as listening to others and
translating content into form.

The eight  chosen designers - Wim Crouwel, Jan van Toorn,
Anthon Beeke, Gerard Hadders, Lies Ros, Lex Reitsma,
Roelof Mulder and Rolf Toxopeus with Wouter van Eyck as
representatives of the Josef Plateau group - were invited
to talk about their view of the profession.

    The participants held discussions with these designers
and later interviewed them, out of which eventually emerged
eight publications - designed by the participants - which have
been brought together in this booklet. The participants - Jop
van Bennekom [Reitsma], Anne Bertus [Ros], Niels Biersteker
[Beeke], Marion Burbulla [Plateau], James Coulson [Crouwel],
Cesare Davolio [Ros], Henk van der Giessen [Mulder and his own
choice: Armand Mevis and Linda van Deursen], Lars Heller
[Hadders] and Elisabeth Pick [van Toorn] - all reacted very
differently to the project. Some ran into difficulties or
prioritised differently in the busy academic schedule, but in
the end everybody invested a lot of energy in it and the long
period of preparation has in the end worked in the project's
favour, a rare advantage in our fast-moving society. The
participants are from Holland, Germany, England, Italy and
Canada. Apart from Cesare Davolio, who joined this project as

a participant from the fine art department with an interest in design, all the participants are graphic designers.

The dualism between theory and practice became clear during the project. The perhaps somewhat vaguely-defined task was given a free, autonomous interpretation, in which the ideas and opinions of the participants were most prominent. Deliberation and co-operation with the invited designers was here and there difficult and was not seen as part of the project. In that sense the Akademie seemed an isolated place without links to the outside world and its (design) history.

The final result of the project, this publication, shows in what way such a task can be worked out: a reduction to the analysis of one design (by Reitsma), a commentary on 'urban visuality', a reflection on the project itself ('Starspotting'), and several interviews which are of interest because of the subjects dealt with; the media, clients from the world of business, the market-oriented economy, the new techniques, the trends and the task of designers in the field of TV and film. We finally opted for a publication in English although for most participants this is not their 'mother tongue'. In particular the interviews and reports of meetings, which were held in English, acquired a special character because of this. We were of the opinion that we should change this as little as possible.

Foretelling the future is an age-old desire, one which remains a rough speculation. But threads can nevertheless be drawn from the past to make assumptions about the future. This project has been concerned mainly with the question as to whether one is conscious of one's profession and its potential. Jan van Toorn (in a recent publication) quoted the communication-scientist Stuart Ewen: 'As we approach the new millennium, the profession of design stands at a fateful juncture. Designers must come to reflect upon the functions they serve, and on the potentially hazardous implications of those functions.' This reflection is necessary; practice will prove to be more difficult.

Robin Kinross
Surveying the scene

The topic is this: where do we stand now, looking around, both
forward to what we can make in the future and back to what has
happened in the past. The generations interact with each other
and each generation itself consists of a continual set of
interactions. Colleagues affect each other, students learn
from each other, students learn from teachers, and teachers
learn from students. Clients and commissioners always have a
decisive role to play in design work. The public is in there
too: somewhere! Then there is the technical realm, and the ways
in which techniques affect what designers do. So it is a matter
of process, rather than of any simple or single development.

Art historians used to make much of 'influence'. How did
this painting come about? They looked for precedents, for
similarity of form in the work of earlier artists, for traits
of style and treatment that suggested development in the
artist. Like Sherlock Holmes, they searched for clues, for
telling details that would yield up secrets. Who were the
artist's teachers? What did Albrecht Dürer see on his trip to
Italy? So one tried to explain and understand an image. But
this still left untouched the question of why. Why did the
painter go on that journey? What was he looking for? What did
he miss in Nuremberg? He was not abducted, but chose to travel
south. Artists choose their influences. They make what they can
of them: taking the things they want, perhaps misunderstanding
and distorting in the process. A trip abroad is certainly one
of the more active steps an artist can take.

So too, time spent in a place such as the Jan van Eyck
Akademie represents a quest: time out from the world of
practice, time spent in reflection and in interaction with
people from other places and other cultures. And this book
provides a set of specific interactions, between designers of
different generations. Yes, a list of subjects was given to
participants. But the participants chose their subjects, and
then represented these subjects as they wished – in dialogue
with those steering the project, and in discussion with their
subjects. The book is a view to the future by means of
interaction: it is an inter-view. So the eight essays that
follow are eight different ways in which such an interaction
can take place.

One could make a sketch of the historical development of the ways in which artists and designers have learnt their trade in Europe and the western world. In the Mediaeval and Early Modern period, one had the informal system of master and apprentice. Skills were passed on in the studio or workshop. Apprentices performed humble tasks, gradually working their way towards independent practice. The world of work was male-dominated; though a familiar move up the scale would happen when the apprentice married the master's daughter. Then came the rise of more formalised, more impersonal knowledge, in academies and similar institutions. The workshop approach was displaced by formal classes, by systems of drawing and of artistic production more generally. Classicism, or rather Neo-Classicism, was instituted. The rules could be articulated and published in handbooks. In the later nineteenth century, this system began to be challenged and broken by avant-garde movements. Painters exhibited outside the established 'salons'. The Arts & Crafts movement attempted to rediscover the workshop principle: to find more authentic, more humane ways of work and production. In the turmoil that followed the end of the Great War of 1914-18, the old world was discredited and its academic model was thrown out. In its place came the modernist attempt to start from scratch, from the most basic and simple things. So, at the Bauhaus in Weimar and then Dessau, students undertook a 'Grundlehre' (foundation course). There was a system here, but there was also the idea that students were in charge of their own destiny. Rather than be inducted into a system of knowledge, young people were seen as having a potential that could be released.

Modernist educational principles later attained wide acceptance in certain places. In the 1960s in Britain, for example, the 'Grundlehre' became a common feature of art and design education. Much of the conflict and trouble within art education in the West in those years revolved around the content of the curriculum, and the extent to which the modernist ideals of free development were being truly realised. With the defeat of radical politics after 1968, one has seen a growing emphasis on the notion that art and design education should be commercially answerable. And this, together with the loss of faith in any set of prevailing assumptions, in any prevailing visual style, is where we are just now.

———

Almost three generations of Dutch graphic design are represented in this book: the post-1945 modernist grandparents, the children who broke with these fathers, and the grandchildren now making their own way. In the old story, sons have to kill off fathers. (Although daughters don't feel such a need to kill mothers?) But this work of parricide becomes difficult to justify rationally when the father has so clearly done some murder himself, as in the case of the generation of Hard Werken and Wild Plakken. What is there left to do in the way of attack? Such a theory may explain the phenomenon of the 'new traditionalism' and the 'new sobriety', or perhaps one should say the 'new new traditionalism' and the 'new new sobriety', whereby designers in their twenties and early thirties have made work that seems more conservative than that of the immediately preceding generation, and which seeks for ordinariness and good manners rather than continual innovation and shock. The most committed of these designers are not represented in this book. Although one can find signs of these attitudes in some of the - to coin a term - 'post-Hard Werken' designers: Lex Reitsma, Mevis and Van Deursen, and Joseph Plateau.

––––––––––

The problem for the sons and the daughters of modernism is that the slaying of the father has already happened. Not just this, but every critical reflection has already been made. Or so it often seems. For example in 1919, the modernist (and Catholic, monarchist, conservative) Anglo-American poet T.S.Eliot, in his essay 'Tradition and the individual talent', argued for the necessity of a critical approach: 'we might remind ourselves that criticism is as inevitable as breathing, and that we should be none the worse for articulating what passes in our minds when we read our book and feel an emotion about it, for criticising our own minds in their work of criticism.' Reflexivity is nothing new, though it is certainly necessary to formulate these ancient ideas in our own words, for our own conditions.

Eliot goes on to outline his theory of tradition: that poets make it new by working within a tradition, by extending and modifying it, so that the old is continually changed by the new. Eliot proposes that the poet ('he') must surrender himself to the work to be done. 'And he is not likely to know what is to be done unless he lives in what is not merely the present, but the present moment of the past, unless he is conscious not of what is dead, but of what is already living.'


## Paul Hefting responds

Dear Robin,

Thanks very much for the fax with your introduction for View to the Future. It is indeed a survey, but a very clear one for this purpose.

The future was always uncertain, but perhaps for other reasons. Also Eliot would have said it now perhaps in other words. The (free) poet must surrender himself to the work to be done... but what work must a designer do? He must work to have a living, dependent on the client, if there is work. I think your introduction asks for reactions and that seems to be a good starting point. I had my own associations, not clear, but rather confused. Nevertheless I send them to you.

Best regards, Paul


I always dream of an article on the iconology of the visual expressions in our time, not only a description of the process, but also of the unknown, but understandable backgrounds of forms (in art, literature and music). So it has been said that the astronomical statement of Copernicus led to the oval in architecture, and Panofsky came to comparable conclusions in different forms of art. It is not easy to relate art and design in our complex world to clear and simple examples in other disciplines. In general, the background is the world we live in (or they lived in): a constant interaction. Dürer went to Italy, not only because of the Renaissance art (of which he would learn the details of perspective), but also for the humanistic ideas, the heritage of the classical world. In comparison to Italy, Germany was in that time rude and still in the Middle Ages. Then a trip abroad was always a voyage to Italy. Also for Dutch artists. Italy was a must. Even in the time of Neo-Classicism.

12

But the industrial revolution, the ideas about economics brought the reactions of the Arts & Crafts-movement, the new ways of painting, music and literature, the new vision of society, in general a reaction against the artificial and against the enormous profits and the even enormous poverty. A protest against the loss of the human. In the twenties the arts again (after 14/18) work with an ideal of a new world, on the other side there is at the same time that disbelieve and mistrust in a real world of justice (DADA etc). Also 1968 had a vision of a new society, better and also more human, but also there was that doubt.

These contrasts are also present in our time, but, as it seems in the western world, no longer relevant. The economy is growing, design is actual, a new fashion. Some voices in the background are protesting against the impersonal and invisable enemy, but weakly, whispering. The voyage to Italy has become a pilgrimage to the Jan van Eyck, where one is protected for two years. No ideal, no clear future, no collective thinking, only the individual thoughts and feelings are important. With some nostalgia artists are referring to tradition, trying to find there a help for a uncertain condition and a vague future of our complex world, in which the economy, marketing, money rule the waves.
     Therefore the Jan van Eyck is a beautiful hiding place, with possibilities for interacting on a small scale, for formulating a possible new ideal. Theory or practice? Clients and commissioners are not allowed in this place. They are too real and can spoil the serene and creative atmosphere. The participants have their criticism, but can it work after the Jan van Eyck? The only thing to do is breathe, and read, hear, listen and react. But somewhere the participants seem to be lost. Is there a possibility for a new tradition? Perhaps the question is how to live, how to be hopeful and how to behave as a human. Difficult task, you can read it in the 'View to the Future'. Every individual participant searched for his/her own point of view. Therefore the booklet will be an illustration of the situation now. But let us be hopeful, this chaos will bring maybe something sublime.

James Coulson
The voice of certainty, the breath of longing

Wim Crouwel

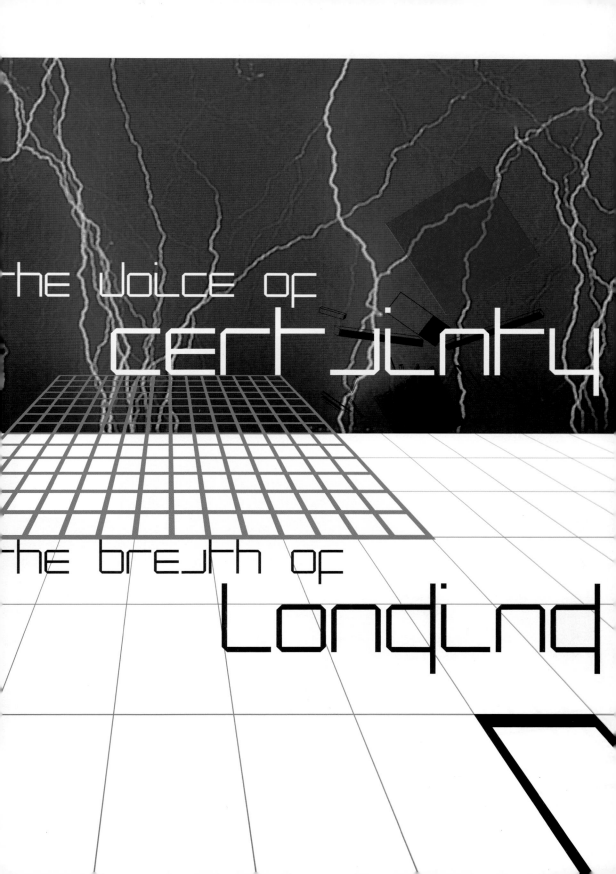

the voice of

certainty

the breath of

Longing

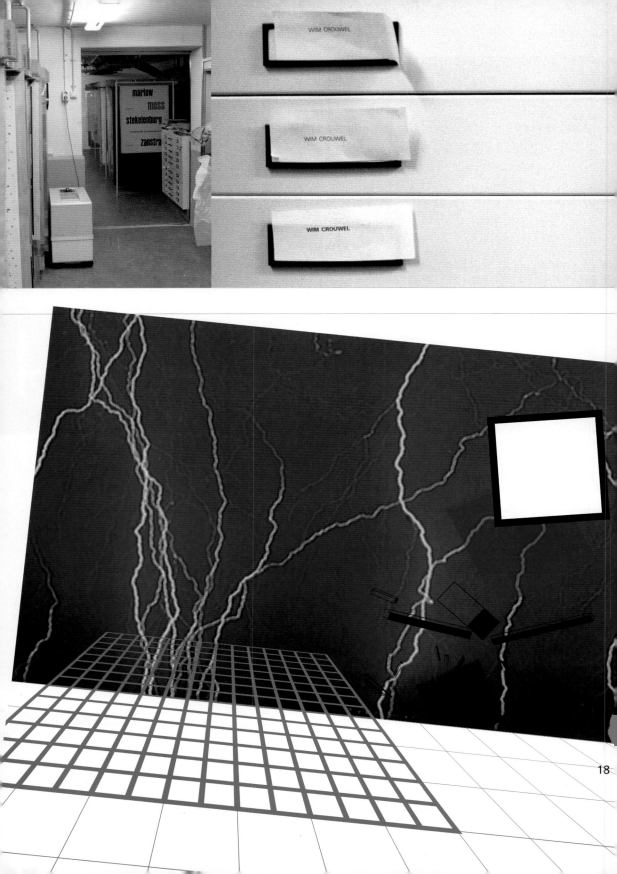

## introduction

Wim Crouwel was born in 1928; he had a general training at the Academy of Arts and Crafts in Groningen between 1946-49 and later specialised in typography at the Institute for Arts and Crafts in Amsterdam 1951-52. In 1963 he became one of five founding partners in Holland's first professional design studio, Total Design (in Amsterdam). Since 1964 he has been responsible for designing many posters, catalogues and exhibitions for the Stedelijk Museum, Amsterdam. Crouwel taught in 's Hertogenbosch [Den Bosch] at the Royal Academy of Arts and Crafts from 1954 until 1957 and at Amsterdam's Institute for Arts and Crafts between 1956 - 1960 and 1962 - 1963. In 1965 he began a long association with Delft University of Technology within the department of industrial design, becoming a professor in 1972. Throughout this period he continued his partnership at Total Design. From 1980 to 1985, Crouwel was involved with the management of the Museum Boymans-van Beuningen in Rotterdam and was advisor for Total Design. In 1985 Crouwel was appointed director of the Museum Boymans-van Beuningen, retiring in 1993.

The examples on the following pages are selected from a range of 355 covers, designed by Wim Crouwel for the Stedelijk Museum, between 1963 and 1984.

1966 Atelier 3

My reason for selecting Wim Crouwel among the o
this publication, is an interest in his adoption of cer
modernist design. Modernism is interpreted in a var
of Modernism in the context of this article is what r

of modernism, nc
advocated so
embraced nev te
of modernism
aesthetics was c
known as 'intern

My former graduate education
at Ravensbourne College of
Design and Communication
spawned an interest in neutrality
in design, especially concerning
typography. The beliefs and
methodologies put forward
by those involved in an
international typographic
approach in many ways
formed the basis of my work.
My interest and adoption
of certain late modernist
ideologies with their objective
and systematic production ethic
concerning clear, effective and
cross cultural communication
played a role in forming my
own design methodology.

Writing a dissertation entitled
'Visual Hermeneutics, Meaning
and Metaphor', had a profound
effect on my views towards
visual communication. My
studies in linguistic theory
and its application to visual
work, have led me to question
my previous views on modernist
attitudes in design. The mass
production ideals of the
modernist movement for
an idealist mass society have,
to a certain extent, failed.
Capitalist society has brought
about a diversification of
markets, a consumer society
where the mass production
of goods and information
has led to the appropriation
of identities by the media.
Modernism's 'machine aesthetic'
now holds less relevance for
a postmodernist audience.
This diversification of markets
and identities has led me to re-
evaluate my ideas about design,
and whether a methodology
as such, should exist.

63|7

esigners chosen for
eologies pertaining to
f ways. My definition
see as the final stage
early avant-garde who
mbolic reform and
ogies, but the tail-end
e, where the use of
in a derivative form
style'.

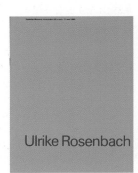

1 Atelier 9        1976 Daniel Buren Hier        1979 Lucassen        1980 Ulrike Rosenbach

The Dutch landscape is like a park. This cultivated a lacks any real countryside. The structured repetition grid-like composition of the land, and the ingenious the North sea from flooding the land, combine to create a safe haven of rationality. The chaos of nature is kept at bay.

The Dutch landscape resembles what Wim Crouwel describes as characteristic of the Dutch people: 'Strict, straightforward, traditional, religious people, not excessive ... "just be normal and it's okay", yet, at the same time, in conflict with a feeling for freedom.'

Wim Crouwel sees himself as an ideal example of the Dutch people. His love of order found it's place within the language of modern design. Crouwel's work, influenced by many modern design ideas, became a modernist hybrid. Important early influences on Crouwel's work were Swiss typographers such as Max Bill, Hans Neuburg and Karl Gerstner. The English designer Anthony Froshaug, who was at the Hochschule für Gestaltung in Ulm, Germany, was also a great influence on Crouwel as a young designer. Crouwel judges his typography as 'somewhere beween the English Modern movement and Swiss design', justifying his looking at foreign influences by saying 'At the beginning of the Fifties there was almost nothing. There was only really classical design and rubbish.'

hundertwasser

When Wim Crouwel completed his general art education in Groningen, he realised that he wanted to be a painter. His expressionist paintings of landscapes, influenced by his fascination with the Dutch landscape, became more abstract. Landscapes began to look like moonscapes. In his paintings the translated abstraction of the Dutch landscapes became more simple, clean, spacious, transparent and geometric.

22

ictly ordered land
es, the almost
s that prevent

swollof mrof
?noij

form follows
{noi?

After specialist training in typography, Wim applied his compositional painting methods to his typography. Wim was intrigued by systematic, clear and minimal design. The grid provided the foundation for his designs. Wim's attitude toward design fell in line with the reductivism of the modernist 'machine aesthetic'. In a semiotic context design meant to 'de-sign'.

Crouwel's ideas ran parallel with a modern design ideology born out of the notion of a 'universal language', known as 'international style'. This language based itself on aesthetic principles of order and a neutral transmission/mediation of information. Page layout was structured with grids, and type usually set in narrow columns ranged to the left, with a sans-serif typeface. Information was laid out objectively. White space became an important consideration in asymmetric layouts. The machine aesthetic, developed on the ideal that 'less is more' supported the notion that design be cleared and emptied of possible variables of meaning.

Crouwel's systematic methodologies concerning hierarchy of information, legibility and neutrality led to an aesthetic synonymous with the 'high' design of modernism. The 'official' design of the Modernist movement resisted pop culture. This was due to a resistance to the unverifiable, the non-rational. People and cultures were addressed as one 'universal' audience, despite varying contexts and histories. The concept of vernacular language was a far cry from the idealists and supporters of 'international style'.

Wim Crouwel's work is an ideal example of this modernist language. However, during the Sixties, Crouwel found that his aesthetic notions conflicted with his functionalist ideals. It would seem that for Crouwel, modernism's idea of 'form follows function' was reversed.

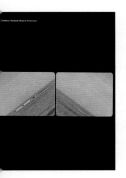

## the utopian square

Wim Crouwel's interpretation of the Modern movement's utopian aesthetic was committed to formal aesthetic notions of order, conflicting with true functionalism. His deep dislike of trends and nature can be seen in his avoiding the use of day-glo colours and his loathing of leaf green, or other 'earthy' colours. A client once insisted on using dark brown, and it made Wim 'absolutely miserable to think about it.'

The utopian square became the utopian aesthetic, cropping information, cropping function. Crouwel said: 'It was the period when I thought I ate only square cookies.

Aesthetics became more important than function for Crouwel, he admits: 'I'm an aesthetic man, I have always said that I'm a functionalist but I am always plagued by my aesthetic system.' His frustration with not being able to use 'ugly' forms such as cutting a rough photograph and pasting it on paper, contradicted his functionalist ideas. This was the case for many of the so-called modernist designers of the 50's and 60's, etc. who mistook aesthetic order for functionalism. Form often became more important than meaning. Crouwel recognises this contradiction: 'Throughout my whole career I was always theorising that things should be clear, straightforward and serve a goal, yet at the same time I discovered that my work is only half-way there, my practical work has such a tendency towards abstraction.'

carel visser

24

Crouwel's work typifies late modernism's resistance to the 'chaos of nature'. Crouwel said 'I have always had a strange feeling for order, that's why I love the Dutch landscape. It's very ordered and very clear. I love that and maybe that's also in my nature. I always wanted to have a clear, straightforward outcome, even if it did not serve the subject.'

The square can be seen as a symbol of modernism. The geometric shape, became the building block for the grid, the grid defined order

I think that the ideas of a utopian aesthetic blocked Wim Crouwel from 'real' functionalist design. Designers such as Crouwel and others of the same period concentrated too much on the structure of form, rather than the production of meaning. Form didn't follow function, function followed form.

the typeface neu alphabet was designed in nineteen sixty seven
wim crouwel designed it as a reaction to the first generation of computer type setting machines
the low resolution of these machines meant that the typefaces became bitmapped crouwels frustration with classical typefaces being spoiled by the machine led him to design a font that would not become bitmapped
the resulting font_ while being a fine example of form and structure_ is less legible than the bitmapped fonts it strived to replace

23.2 tm 8.4.79
extra bulletin
stedelijk museum
amsterdam
bazaine

neu
alphabet

25

In order to put Wim's ideologies in the context of today's audience, I will try to use my own experience to explain why I feel the modern language of the 'international style' fails to address differing audiences' experiences of consuming information.

Today, the notion of a universal aesthetic to deliver information is impossible. This is due to our consciousness of the increasingly heterogeneous structure of audiences, existing in the world, each with their own aesthetic codes. In order to speculate about these audiences, one can look to new generations: I will examine a youth culture market which is often referred to as the 'MTV generation'.

This new generation consumes information in a variety of ways, fuelled by diverse subcultures and new technologies, built up through global mass consumption and mass markets asking for a diversification of products. Brought up on computers as the norm, users plug into highly developed entertainment software. Information is presented in forms where a variety of senses are stimulated, heightening the experience of consuming information.

Music plays an important role in the development of youth culture. Information can be carried in a more usable state. Lyrical content found in music such as Hip-Hop became an information system for discontented youth during the Eighties. The music, mainly sampled from Seventies funk, became the carrier of socio-political concerns to a generation lacking representation in mass media. A younger generation consumed information through various stimuli of the senses.

This so-called 'MTV Generation' consumes information at breakneck speed, collecting sound-bites. With information speeding up through the use of various media, a generation can lose its concentration. This lack of discipline can make lengthy books seem dull. Books now seem distant to a younger generation. Texts that deal at length with one idea seem tiresome to a generation who consume 'bites' of information, in the form of various sense-stimulating media. Not only is this due to length, but also the use of language. Books use vernacular that seems 'academic' to a generation who do not read.

One example of the function of targeted vernacular text can be observed in the popularity of Irvine Welsh's book (and film) Trainspotting. Set in Glasgow, Scotland, the book follows the antics of friends, dealing with the issue of heroin abuse. A factor that makes Irvine Welsh's novel different from other authors is his strong use of vernacular language. Glaswegian street slang in its stronge form, combined with its controversial content an honest representation of youth culture mad Trainspotting a best-seller.

For certain new generations, writing nowada is usually digested in the form of subcultur magazines and fanzines. Ray Gun magazine (LA base music magazine) cornered part of this market with circulation of around 120,000 copies per month. Ra Gun's popularity is obviously due to the design David Carson's input. Carson became identified as rebel against conventional magazine design. Desig purists (what's left of the modernist old schoo cringed at such a confused, illegible layout. Carsor guiding philosophy is 'responding emotionally', in h words, to the subject matter. In an interview in Th Guardian International (1 May 1996, Page 8 of suppl ment) after being questioned about 'his old friend the writers being happier with a more sober design', Carson said 'I'll tell you what the real disservice to writing is - just taking copy and laying it out neutrally. I read the articles, get the tone, interpret it.' The Guardian journalist responded with 'But how about letting the writing do the work itself?' Carson said 'Ah, well, this is where the confusion lies. You all think that writing is the  king, but I'm a visual journalist. Designers are trad tionally meant to serve... but I'm not a servant.'

What the critics of Ray-Gun failed to recogni was that the new generation didn't necessarily want read the text but preferred to read images. Te became image for most of its audience, yet offere readability for those who could be bothered. It could b argued that such a confused, illegible layout masks th fact that Ray-Gun magazine was poorly written. Carso was probably aware of this, yet by stating that he is visual journalist Carson is declaring that the forms use provide arguments about the world. Yet under exam nation it would seem that the formal quality of th work will often lend itself to formal rhetoric instead information through aesthetics. A designer/auth mediates information. Carson often destroys it, in ord to create an aesthetic of identity. This identity is the ke to Ray-Gun's popularity. The function of the magazi is often to present an identity for a market to relate t for people who just want to 'join the club', actual info mation exchange is a low priority.

The question of designers as visual authors, determining their own content, was put to Wim Crouwel, who responded with 'I think it's nonsense! That's what designers should not do... Designers are intermediaries between someone who has to say something and someone who has to read it.' Crouwel's views are based on his ideology of neutral design. The argument for neutrality as a non-mediator of information has been exposed as a false one under Postmodern critique. With the diversification of audiences, the argument for neutrality in design holds no weight. Modernism's preoccupations with form and ignorance of the production of meaning within a social/cultural context is the background to Crouwel's belief that designers serve as neutral deliverers of information.

The identities created through diversification of markets by the media are embedded with aesthetic codes, codes which are signifiers of meaning, opening up interpretation to the audience. Crouwel's idea of non-mediation is based on the modernist communication model of client-designer-audience, with the designer adding extraneous meaning. A postmodern perspective sees the communicative model as a circular relationship between client, designer and public. The designer cannot be a neutral mediator as the message must be interpreted, the designer cannot avoid interpretation. The designer's background determines his/her interpretation, and while this background is likely to run parallel with that of the clients, practice now demands that the designer develops a consciousness of their own position within this system. In a postmodern society where many 'truths' exist modernist design methodology becomes just another style or 'truth'.

Though Carson termed his style 'the end of print', Ray-Gun spawned many imitations. Magazines around the world have appropriated Carson's style in order to gain popularity and sales. In the UK, MTV and the publishers of Ray Gun conceived a new magazine aimed at the youth culture of Britain - BLAH, BLAH, BLAH'. Taking over where Carson left off, the text 'the rebirth of print' can be read in its tattered masthead.

Despite the fact that Carson's style is illegible, it does manage to communicate impressionistically. Modernist design provides a systematic container for reading long lengths of text but falls short in providing impressionistic communication. This new design invites the user to construct his/her own meaning which might induce a more intuitive response to the information. The new generation is understood to read less linearly than modernists imagined of their audiences. Meaning can be determined through formal expression, as well as reading text. Magazines for the youth culture market are more and more needing to cater for a 'soundbite' audience. Often many pages need to introduce and illustrate an article's idea. Magazines such as Wired will often employ a chaotic, layered, visually rich illustration of text and image, in order to entice the reader. Yet the actual articles are usually presented in a reduced visual, classical layout. Youth culture magazines which value the content of their writing are having to cater for identity markets. By attempting to supply an identity for markets which want to 'join the club' and also markets which are genuinely interested in the content, a compromise is often arrived at. This seems to be the case for many youth culture magazines. In Britain, The Face deals with text traditionally, (through columns on a grid) along with other visual ways of dealing with information. The magazine works on various visual levels. A lot of space is given to images and large quotes, so that the reader can easily leaf through the pages and get a good understanding of what each article is about. In this context, the face is truly a functionalist design, as it allows the reader fast non-linear access to articles which may be of interest.

Another interesting way of dealing with issues is by making 'funky'-looking diagrams that deal with observations about certain social concerns. In the April (1996) issue, The Face dealt with the subject of illegal sexual acts around the world in the form of a world map with graphic symbols, in a dance music type of vernacular. In the May (1996) issue The Face experimented with the psychology of reading children's drawings by playing various styles of music from contemporary artists to five and six year-olds, and asking them to draw and write about what the tracks made them think of. Another way of presenting information that The Face seems fond of is to display viewpoints, usually from different subcultures, in the form of a chart. Different questions are asked to each person and then displayed using vertical and horizontal axes (x,y) to present the information (which is usually in small quotes, soundbites or symbols). Also when dealing with headings and sub-headings, The Face will usually quote lyrics from a pop song that reinforce the article's content. This shows a relating of music to youth culture; a recognised language through lyrics from music that speaks to an audience who knows such lyrics.

The strong link of music to youth culture can be seen in the marketing strategies of companies such as MTV, who are fully aware of the need to market their product by tailoring aesthetics and language to a certain audience, often referred to as 'generation x' or 'slackers'. Young people, disgruntled because of low employment and pessimistic about the future, now have a lot more leisure time on their hands. MTV knows this, offering an identity that instills a sense of pride in such a lifestyle. The following refers to the postcard pictured. 'Home is chilling out', sets the premise for a nation who spends more time at home in front of the TV, signified in the phrase 'couch potato'. The ironic use of modern vernacular language used for selling products, such as 'machine-washable, fat-free TV addiction' pretends to treat its targeted audience with an understanding of their pessimistic view on society and modern-day living. This use of language, coupled with the aesthetics of an orange retro couch and fur rug reminiscent of the Seventies, reinforces home and leisure time, while hinting at a style-conscious viewer.

Through briefly looking at print geared towards youth culture, it can be concluded that new generations have not changed their reading habits. Magazines just have to work a lot harder to entice some readers. This need to identify with aesthetic codes is partly where modernism's preoccupation with neutrality, ignoring the production of meaning, failed to serve an audience. Information presented to, and targeted at, differing subcultural groups needs to be tailored to suit a particular audience's reading habits.

Wim Crouwel's p
researches the qu
to be critical of th
pragmatic, they c

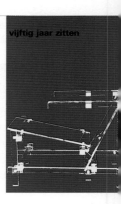

# design education

·n as chairman of the Visitatie Commissie, which
of all art schools in Holland, places him in a position
ucation system. 'Students today are much more
e teachers who are not critical. In the Seventies
people loved soft-talking, they
didn't like criticism, but it's a
completely different situation
today and I'm afraid that most
teachers are always one step
behind and that's a tragedy.

**g. rietveld architect**

It would also seem to be the case that in many educational institutions students tend to learn more from each other. 'Students are much more critical of each other than the teachers are,' argues Wim. He also concludes that '... younger teachers are better in an art school. I always think that there should be very young teachers, and they should not have contracts for a long period, five years should be the maximum.'

Teaching methodologies are also scrutinised by Crouwel, 'I do not have a clear idea of what should be the model for the future, I only want to present it here as a question. In most educational institutes and academies where designers are educated, the main emphasis is on the idea, the idea is the most important thing and the final result is not so important anymore.' This would seem to be a valid point. Educational establishments reacting against the superficiality of the 'Eighties' seem now to be concentrating on ideas or 'concepts'. Function is secondary. Whereas the modern movement tried to concentrate on form following function, postmodern education of the Nineties seems to concentrate on function following concept.

I believe that for an educational model of the future, institutions should concentrate on the function of design. Only after researching the purpose of the communication as far as the consumer of the information is concerned, can a communication strategy be applied. In a postmodern society where subcultural groups become more diverse, the need for 'tailor-made' or 'targeted' communication becomes apparent. This can be made possible by a methodology based on the marketing strategy of advertising.

29

Through examining my own experience of trying to
and by speaking to Wim Crouwel about his ideolog
that today such a methodology fails. The sterility of
a variety of subcultures. Aesthetic codes of languag
should be employed as part of the communication

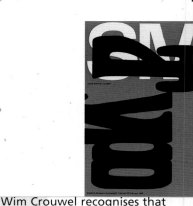

Wim Crouwel recognises that design groups such as 8v0 (whom he employed for the Boymans-van Beuningen in Rotterdam, whilst he was director) serve a particular role and 'for specific clients they do the job very well.' Whereas such design groups set out with the notion of a derived universal language, they are now finding themselves restricted to a particular subcultural group.

The mass communication ideal of the Modern movement seems to be defunct. In a postmodern society, the machine aesthetic of modernism becomes 'just another style', a style that can be used in varying contexts. In America it is usually identified as 'corporate style', in England a neo-modernism aesthetic has become synonymous with dance music, probably due to its 'machine aesthetic' representing advances in new technology employed by dance music.

30

ise neutral, systematic design
have come to the conclusion
iversal language' fails to attract
t vary between subcultures
ss. The result would hopefully
become a more meaningful
xperience and further
nhance the function
f the communication.

The 'high' design ethic of late modernism acted as a religion for many designers. Crouwel talks of it as '... a belief... it is absolutely religion. People can never get rid of their religious ideas.' When talking of Antony Froshaug, Crouwel said 'he was a great friend of mine, he was also a kind of religious priest to me... he couldn't work for industry or anything like that, of course not... but he was a great teacher and clergyman' (Crouwel laughs).

Talking of designers as 'cultural chameleons', Crouwel said 'I know designers who have a very different approach, designers who try to find a different solution for every commission they get, who are flexible and who have no specific style, and I think in future this will be more and more the case.' Crouwel is keen to point out that he hates this idea. He concludes: 'We need designers who can solve a problem... It's a completely different type of designer from me, completely different... But please, designers with a view!'

The problem remains: how does a designer communicate to anyone beyond their own subculture? The cultural appropriation by mainstream design of the vernacular has problematic social implications. The use of a vernacular may result in a designer unwittingly patronising and displaying naivety towards differing social groups using inevitable communicative clichés. In extreme cases this could cause cultural exclusion, heightening the possibilities of stereotyping between subcultures. It would seem that there are two options here: either the designer practises and communicates to people who are within a similar subcultural grouping, or he/she invests time in research in order to act as a 'cultural chameleon'.

## conclusion

gerry
schum

1980 Gerry Schum          1977 Japanese affiches

Wim Crouwel's fight with aesthetics and function left him feeling that 'as a designer I was always theorising that things should be clear, straight forward and serve a goal. But I discovered that my work was only half-way there, my practical work had such a tendency towards abstraction, there is a very strange contradiction in my whole career.'

## Crouwel has always been pro-clarification of information

Crouwel's honesty in recognising the trappings of an ideology on which he based most of his career as a graphic designer is testament to his openmindedness and enthusiasm for design serving a social function. Crouwel was always pro-clarification of information, it's just that he seemed to get caught up in a religious ideology which didn't recognise different audiences or the forms that spoke to them. Crouwel concludes: 'I am not religious, I'm a real socialist absolutely on the left.'

Elizabeth Pick
'<u>Everything you always wanted to know about
reflexivity but were afraid to ask</u>'

Jan van Toorn

# "Everything you always wanted to know about reflexivity but were afraid to ask."

AN INTERVIEW WITH JAN VAN TOORN BY
ELIZABETH PICK, MARCH 4, 1996

WARNING:
THIS ARTICLE CONTAINS IDEAS WHICH MAY BE
HARMFUL TO THOSE WHO WISH TO PROTECT
THEIR  POSITION IN THE STATUS QUO.

elizabeth pick How does reflexivity work? jan van toorn Human beings reflect upon their activity. Culture reflects on its activity and upon its being, the human condition. Consider the history of design, architecture, fine art, it's not only that we make things but that it's constantly being reflected upon by artists, architects and designers, and also by others. There is a theoretical discourse that exists related to our activity. ep Is there a lack of thinking amongst designers? jvt There is not a lack of thinking but people don't admit that they think. They always say, 'I make, so sorry don't ask me what it means,' which was very typical in the discussion with Wim Crouwel for example. If you ask why do you use a certain colour or a certain type? The answer is mostly 'well, that's personal.' We are creating truth by our actions all the time. In the visual culture in general you can see that there is a tradition that wants to go with the dream, the materialising of the dream, of ethical and aesthetic principles. People base their action in one way or another on that dream, and they try to make it fit reality learning that it will never fit. In the making, in the reality of life, things are more complicated. ep Is it used as a kind of motivation? jvt Yes, and even people who deny that they use it, do.

## Reflexivity is a notion for me which has to do with the human condition, that you strive for something (even when you deny it).

ep Even when you know you can't attain it? jvt Yes, of course, otherwise there is no life, that's very simple. In philosophy you find people like Ernst Bloch who give it a name, the 'principle of hope'. It is a very primary thing. It has to do with the strategy of realising your ideological agenda in practice. The more radical the ideas are, the more influence they will have on your action. ep How specific is this to the condition of designers? It sounds like this type of thinking is applicable to every profession. jvt It is, but you should make a difference between two main streams in cultural activity. To use politics again for example, conservatives say life is as it is. For them it is a natural condition and there is no point considering any other value systems or social order. The others criticise the existing order and values and try to realise their ideals. They develop strategies for communication about alternatives which leads us to the arts in general and to design. There, practical intellectuals develop new models and commentaries that have a very strong influence on our relationship to the world. In film, in literature, in theatre, architecture, and fine art you find this self-conscious genre well articulated and also well developed as a means of communication and expression. This is important to remember, especially because we are living in a society that in the last twenty years has accepted the socio-cultural condition we live in as given by nature.

jvt One of the problems I'm faced with and try to think about is that design has lost its perspective and means of contributing to a better world. So many intellectuals are frustrated because of the developments in the last century. It's very understandable because designers and architects in particular have to answer to the market, which means accommodating the established powerful interests.

jvt The most typical characteristic in a reflexive work is that it always exposes itself as an interpretation. That is fundamental in the reflexive tradition. The familiar tradition always deals with objective representation and never exposes itself.

jvt Living means being moralistic. All communication is interpretation otherwise there is no communication. There is no neutrality, you always try to communicate something of your being in relationship to the existing cultural background. What is important also is how you think about your relationship to the other as a communicator. It is typical that the modernist tradition in practice ended up having a very patriarchal approach to the audience and thought about communication as a neutral and linear form of transmission from one to the other. That's not what the independent formation of opinion is about in a democratic sense, and that's something we should strive for with all that we have. I think all opposition in human history has to do with an open and interpretative attitude to the use of language.

jvt When you reflect critically on your position as a human being and in the social context you shouldn't see that as an enormous frustration, but rather accept that reality and develop a strategy according to your own agenda. It could be in one case leaning more towards official design standards and in other cases it could be more radical. That's what the life of a practitioner is about. Don't escape into artistic arguments about independence with the illusion that you are an objective mediator, that only becomes a pain in your soul.

jvt The best example of conventional representation by design can be found in the Dutch passport. Like the general representation of the family, Dutch history is presented in a stereotypical way. It's really very hard to find a designer with a different attitude, someone who deals with the world in a less conventional way. You can hardly find one dissident designer at the moment. What I'm missing are the real outside voices. Only someone like Rem Koolhaas is really developing an idea of the world that questions the established order.

*jvt*

*The constructivists were an elite. The change in society was a result of a failing system and was made by others but the ideas for the new order were already expressed by the elite. The elite classes are disciplining the world together with established regimes which force other people to deal with the world in the way they think about it. In a symbolic sense we see reality as articulated by the elite not by the people.*

The renewal of thinking is always created by the intellectuals and the change of material conditions is made by the people. Thinking about culture takes place in social groups connected with the establishment. They have the time, the education and the places in which to do it. What is very typical for design today is that it is so accommodating, so affirmative. My own teachers, Charles Jongejans and Lex Metz who were students of Piet Zwart, Paul Schuitema and also Willem Sandberg, were great examples after the second world war of designers trying to tell us that critical reflection on the social conditions creates the distance necessary for cultural renewal. They tried to make clear which strategies they used and how they were organised to realise their contribution to better living conditions in a material and spiritual way. They were very open about their aesthetic and political strategies. This was an important part of my education but several years later I rebelled precisely against the result of their striving because most of them identified themselves too much with mass production and consumption which ended up in a basic aesthetic seen everywhere in the world.

jvt There was a revival in the Sixties of critical thought which was accompanied by strong politics of operational critique. This has a very long tradition beginning before the start of the Jewish and Christian religions. One can see this striving for a better world in all kinds of libertarian philosophies of life, in our lifetime or after. Throughout the ages you can also see how the waves of each revolution go over the top and new regimes of control establish themselves.

Italian film and the French 'nouvelle vague' are based on storytelling and language use of an author's position, which you relate to as a viewer, with possibilities for interpretation and understanding. It is less illusionistic. In Shakespeare and Cervantes, you find many examples of this narrative method, such as the court jester who winks to the audience to show that it is a 'made thing' which is not natural and therefore does not need to be naturalistic.

*It is essential in the reflexive tradition that you know that the message is stemming from somebody, and that it invites you and forces you to relate the story to your own experience and history, and not to be distracted because there is this attractive illusion which only you can consume.*

*<sub>jvt</sub> The role of the intellectual demands an awareness of the consequences of acting in an environ- ment that establishe. a disciplinary order in co-operation pow- erful social groups.*

ep With reference to the different waves which you mentioned, where are we now? And with a View to the Future, where are we going? jvt Now we are in a kind of a phase, especially in design, of enormous changes in media and production. In general I think it's a transitional period we're living in, an extremely capitalist one where communications are controlled by huge corporations, by military and state organisations. The images of the world are extremely one-dimensional and favour the existing power system. The threats to social and natural environments all over the world are not there by accident. This question with a View to the Future for me means we should go back to fundamental problems of poverty and disinformation which people have experienced for ages. All technological developments are sold to us as tools for progress. When you talk about communication that, for me, should be something that deals with independent information and participation of the people. What's sold to us as improvement or liberty is even more of a conservative revolution because it does not consider the participation of the hundreds of millions of people in the world in their own development. We as designers tend to believe the virtual hype which is sold to us by the corporate take-over of public media. The problem of communication in the future is hardly discussed in a genuine democratic sense. So what we do is forced on us by production circumstances of the market and we produce more and more affirming information in new settings.

ep When is the next boiling point going to happen? jvt Now that we are more or less in a period where we can see that this can't go on we must think about operational possibilities for reflexive practitioners. There are large spaces and needs outside of the market. Our critique and uneasiness should be articulated in very practical approaches. If you don't seriously analyse what is wrong with the world, you will never be able to deal with substantial themes or subjects. This kind of fundamental reflection on culture is necessary to develop a programme for action. When you think about a concrete project according to that programme it should happen in a critical way because today's confirmation does not work, that should help you find new ways of giving it form. We don't train ourselves in the grammar of the reflexive practices anymore. We are educated in formal aesthetics and functionalistic behaviour. I think you now see design and architecture going back to these. For me that's a reaction to postmodernist pluriformity. That's for me rather a conservative not to say fundamentalist approach. I want to measure it by the way it deals with the public. I hope for a more democratic basis for participation and emancipation.

ep Are the possibilities in making also involving the changing of the production relationships?
jvt Very difficult. My favourite example is the stamp for the hundredth birthday of Dutch prime minister Drees. What happened was, Ootje Oxenaar, the commissioner, was thinking about Drees in the same way as I was. He was emotional about it because Drees was a social democrat responsible for the colonial war in Indonesia. We were both in opposition to that policy which was a rather isolated position at that time. The first thing I thought about was to expose Mr. Drees as the defender of the Dutch colonial empire. I did a sketch of a burning Indonesian village, knowing that it would never be accepted by the Dutch PTT. So that's a good example of how you could do that to the extreme. The other proposal was

to try to show Mr. Drees as he saw himself. He is not only responsible for the colonial war but also for the introduction of the social security system. He saw himself as the father of the Dutch people. He was simple, he didn't spend money, he walked to work, he played [Dutch] baseball with his family in the dunes on Sundays. I was looking for a photograph that would represent him as he presented himself and combine that with the colours of his coalition government. I also made it informal by bending the photograph. I chose an official photograph from the Dutch government's public relations department but the proposal was not accepted by the cabinet of the prime minister because a prime minister could not be represented lying in the dunes. That was the official reason but actually it exposed a duality in the behaviour of Mr. Drees as a politician. It relativised Mr. Drees as a national hero and showed him being aware of his public role. A careful construction, deconstructed by the design. ep Is the fact that it was not accepted but generated a valuable process and discussion also satisfying? jvt I would have loved to have had that one accepted of course...

*Another thing which I discussed with Ootje was that I wouldn't represent Mr.Drees as a person like the queen, visually cut his head off and make him an icon. The universal icon at one end and the subjective interpretation at the other, and within that range you have endless possibilities.*

*The most important point for us to agree upon was that he should not be represented as a person above all parties. He was a typical social democrat who strove for consensus. A politician who represented middle class values.*

ᵉᵖ The stamp that was made, do you consider that a compromise? ʲᵛᵗ I don't see it as a compromise. I had to go a little further in the direction of the pure icon but without going there completely. My next step was to choose a photograph of the moment Drees went to the Dutch parliament with the social security act in his briefcase. What I tried to do was look for a photograph which showed him as an official person and still use colour pointing to the coalition government. I used unusual elements (numbers and cropping) to make it a more vernacular design but I had to find what I wanted mostly in more formal solutions rather than in the meaning of the photo. ᵉᵖ Were you working in co-operation with the commissioner or is your commissioner allowing you to work independently in this way? What kind of partnership is it when you can make those kinds of commentaries? How much autonomy does a designer have? Can you work without an enlightened commissioner? ʲᵛᵗ No, its absolutely necessary, but even when you don't have an enlightened commissioner, in principle you have to negotiate to create the space to make the same kind of choices.

ootje oxenaar (25.3.96) *'When I think of the role of van Royen, and Kröller Müller, in my opinion it was the commissioners who had the idea of asking Berlage, to ask Mondriaan, to ask Doesberg, and Van der Lek to decorate their new hunting mansion, to have fantastic printed material, and later to commission good designers. In the case of the PTT it was Van Royen who had the social ideas. He believed a labourer had the right to a good chair, table, and good surroundings. That of course was based on making more money because when the labourer is happy, he works better and you get more profit out of him. But in the beginning these were socialist ideas. When Van Royen came into the PTT he thought he would put these ideas into practice. It was good for the company, good for the workers, and the state could provide an example of how things could be. In turn it stimulated the arts. So everything was fine and everyone was happy and in the meantime he organised and united the artists, designers and craftsmen. He also had his little printing works at home which was very inspirational for him. The initiative for the creative people to go on working that way was the commissioner's, but he could not do anything if he could not find artists and designers who could think for themselves.'*

In making, are you holding up a mirror image of the world to show and manifest reality or a new image to identify with? jvt El Lissitsky saw his exhibitions as an argument but he was also aware of their propagandist value. In the famous Cabinet for Fine Art in Hanover he tried to show works of art, Mondriaan, Kandinsky etc. in such a manner that people had the opportunity to react and participate in the ideas. He did not want to present them as a kind of canonical and universal truth. His critique of Le Corbusier's approach was fundamental in saying that the way he concentrated on the aesthetics of architecture was very much related to his authoritarian ideas about the city and living. Thus he created sophisticated environments that separated their inhabitants from the social and cultural reality in which they lived. His exhibitions have much more to do with trying to argue and to tell, instead of trying to convince by aesthetic means. The role of a designer is not primarily pointed to aim for an aesthetic result but for a communicative one based on participation, and for a learning process that allows people to participate and form an opinion based on how they encounter the world. ep How are your ideas about reflexivity and all these other ideas we've talked about different from what you thought in the 70s? How have your ideas developed and how have they changed?

jvt I was much more naive, particularly concerning factors such as production circumstances and the function of the public sphere. You learn all the time. I have more theoretical insight now as well as practical experience. Here at the Jan van Eyck in the last five years I learned a lot about the tools of thinking and about how other people deal with the same questions. When I started to work for the Van Abbemuseum Jean Leering had a clear idea about the public role of the museum as a mediator. I was thinking more out of a reaction to official design which Wim Crouwel represented with its functionalist approach, that it should be less institutional. We used the more popular design idiom to express this other attitude. Over a period of 10 years we developed in much more depth the ideas about a mediator's role in information. There were also political aspects affecting the process. In the beginning we were only thinking of a style approach that expressed something of our discontent but very slowly, by working and reflecting upon the results, we saw that it wasn't important anymore to have a coherent stylistic alternative. We came to the conclusion that once there was a mentality, an identity, form would develop out of the choices that were made. The concern wasn't the style anymore, but rather how to articulate curatorial and editorial considerations in the best visual and spatial way. That's something we didn't formulate before but we experienced and discovered while we were working. So when you look back and say there was a style, it's not coherent as a kind of system that's a construction in itself but rather the outcome of a process.

*jvt It's a very basic way of learning. It took me some time to overcome the liberal idea that when you mirror the world in its complexity you represent reality in the best way.*

... Designers need good reasons to get up out of bed in the morning. Believing in and striving for utopias seem to be as good a reason as any but the almighty dollar, or guilder in the case of the Netherlands, seems to be the motive of choice. All professionals find themselves at some point facing a moral dilemma about how they position themselves in relation to the world and designers are no exception. However, designers hold a dubious position as members of the media so their moral dilemma becomes so much the greater because of the potentially large visibility of their work. This personal responsibility is articulated in several ways because designers are responsible for, among other things, visualising reality.

A growing trend in representation in the media is the 'add a minority and stir' approach. Images of black men in business, Asian women in medicine and all colours of children huddled around their computers oblivious of their differences and engrossed in learning can be found in stock photography catalogues. Using these images eases the conscience but does it get any closer to real representation?

The stock photo books also offer a cornucopia of images ranging from idealised versions of the state of our environment to perfect picture postcard images of the world's cities that no tourist or resident has ever experienced. There seems to exist genuine confusion when trying to represent reality, and designers who generally come from white middle class backgrounds have a hard time representing any realities other than their own. Even the representation of women and minorities is circumspect because only when they were discovered to make up a large part of the consumer market were they used.

The stock photography industry is immense and the amount of images used from these books in the media completely overshadows the efforts of the earnest graphic designer struggling to balance his or her version of reality with their client's needs. The use of stock images originated in the United States and has developed in the last forty years into an integral part of the Dutch media. One only has to glance through the brochures at the Dutch PTT or the ABN-AMRO bank stands to appreciate the scale of their spread. Not only are the images trying to break away from only depicting white males in positions of authority but at the same time they contain a unique American perspective seen in everything from hairstyles to body language. The Dutch reality is once again blurred.

Instead of pointing a finger at the stock photography industry perhaps it is more fruitful to question the reasons for its success. These images of so-called artificial life are used because they work. They present a different utopia to which the Dutch dreamer in the street can aspire instead of the utopias of trying to create a better world. The difference in motivation is great but the root is similar. The stock photo image with its smiling healthy people, multi-racial friendships, clean cities and good life ask of people in theory to realise that they don't belong to this Disneyland dream and to act and react in the best of the reflexive tradition ...- elizabeth pick

Niels Biersteker
<u>Interview to the future</u>

Anthon Beeke

INTER
VIEW
TO THE
1996
FUTURE

business man. He's a very good message-artist and he's not a designer. So he never feels guilty. That's absolutely true! Of course he is a designer, but not the designer everybody thinks he is. (G.H.:'He's an editor designer, a strategist.') And that's completely different from other designers, that makes him very strong.

G.H.  Yes, because you don't have to cut yourself off from your own product, so to speak, you don't experience the pain which that causes. It's a very made thing. Management is something you should know about, but you should go to a business school to learn that, really, and not to an art school. There is always some sacrifice involved, meaning that if someone is doing very well creatively (the 'Peter principle'), he usually becomes a manager of a group of people, and after that he is either a bad manager or a bad designer. It's absolutely impossible to be both at the same time.

**A.B.*** Anthon Beeke
**A.B.** Anne Bertus
**D.B.** Dawn Barret
**J.B.** Job van Bennekom
**N.B.** Niels Biersteker
**S.B.** Samira Benlaloua

**G.H.** Gerard Hadders
**P.H.** Paul Hefting
**K.M.** Karel Martens
**F.S.** Femke Snelting
**R.T.** Renée Turner
**X.X.** Unidentified

*Excerpts from an interview held at the Jan van Eyck Akademie, Maastricht 6-12-96 Photography by Frank van Helfteren*

# Old and new news

D.B.  Both of you are managers, designers and educators, what are the differences?

G.H.  If you're in education, the student is your main concern. If you are working with an employee, the job is your main concern. The development of any 'thing' requires a sacrifice. That is of course the interesting aspect of the Cranbrook method that Dumbar introduced; you let most of your designers work freely (up to a point) and then you start editing the product. I think that is a very rare situation.

A.B.*  Gert is able to do that. He's an educator to his clients, not to the people in his studio. He believes in design, and he's a very good

A.B.*  Once, I made an alphabet of nude girls, do you remember?

D.B. ——————— I do, yes.

A.B.*———————  The lithographer was a guy from Switzerland. The Steendrukkerij De Jong, the first printer in the Netherlands, produced this publication, de Kwadraatbladen, and they sent me to Switzerland. We were talking about the quality of lithography in Holland and he said: 'The Dutch people are as good as we are, and sometimes better. But the quality is not consistent; the problem is that the best lithographer in Holland became a studio manager. And so you get a lousy studio manager and you've lost your best lithographer. Here we pay more, and hire a good studio manager.'

D.B.  It ends up being a question of productivity, if you're managing 20 people, more is being produced. That's why you're getting paid, even

# Personal critique

*(special issue)*

Anthon Beeke, one of the most well known figures in Dutch graphic design, has been around since the early days of this profession; he experienced the birth of a new direction after the Arts and Crafts movement and has taken part in the changes up to now. Without any academic baggage he started working for Ed Callahan, Jacques Richez and Jan van Toorn, who taught him on the job. After starting up his own studio ('62-'63), he was soon invited to become a teacher at the academies in Den Bosch and Enschede (and later at the Rietveld). Although he's most

ly different attitude. They all think Holland is the 'Biebelebonseberg' ['heaven', from nursery rhyme] and that something happened in 1512...and...1512, yes, 1512, or is it 1513, professor? 1572, 1572! 14!

G.H.   It's not only over, I think it never existed.

D.B.   Wooh! There was a comfortable time here!

G.H.   But for whom?

D.B.   OK, it was limited, but there was a comfortable period of about 8 years. How different is it for this generation, is it a closed world?

famous

though the end result is not as good.

G.H.   But I do think that art schools should pay attention to general aspects of marketing and communication. This is not done at all (most of the time). A brief introduction to these things, before you enter a market (...) I really think it is an important thing. If you think your work is important, you must be able to defend it on levels other than your particular, personal one. You need an introduction. They give these basic courses in marketing for non-marketeers.

D.B.   Have you ever taken one?

G.H.   I learned it the hard way. Anthon has been part of that world since the 60's. It's a different attitude. The situation in Holland, so young designers seem to think, is that somewhere there is a secret pool of money that will provide them with enough funds to continue their freewheeling. (...)

A.B.*   I agree with Gerard. In other countries that feeling was already there.
Designers from France, Germany, Switzerland, England and the United States have a complete-

G.H.   I think the field has become much wider, maybe it feels like a closed world, but there's one way forward and that's to get interested in analysing it. Don't stay on the outside. You have to read magazines, visit people. You also have to read the economics section, and you have to read the trade papers. It's not like going to the Stedelijk [Stedelijk Museum, Amsterdam] to see another revolutionary French designer exhibited there. It's more to do with this other aspect. You have to create -like fine artists do- a strategy and a plan which runs for at least two years. That's something that's not necessary if you happen to be in the situation where you get picked out, as happened to Anthon, and myself maybe, although we were both developing things before that happened. The best strategy is to start up something that goes beyond design. Because, to be pretty blunt, I think design in itself is less than zero. You can also prove yourself as a designer if you go beyond design. The moment at which you become your own client is always the most interesting. This time is as good as any other to start something like that. And now we have things like the Internet, which provides an opportunity to enter a base platform (which in the old days we

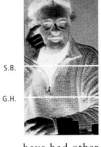

would call a client) practically free. Something that in the old days would have cost a lot of money.

**S.B.**  **I am surprised, it looks like a very negative situation.**

**G.H.**  It is. It's quite simple, there are more and more people in the field. I think that when Anthon started, there were 1% of the designers that there are now, and when I started, 10%. The market is also growing, but it is full of other people, people who have had other kinds of education. That's the important thing.

It has to do with professionalisation of this trade. There are clients we both dealt with, where previously you would have had one person wearing three different hats, and now you have a different person for each hat. It has become more complicated, but the reference material they work with is much more simple, and they all come from the same school.

**P.H.**  And I also ask myself whether, when you began, the climate was influenced by other things, like dada and fluxus. A new field of inspiration. I think that what was inspiring for the 60's had nothing to do with design.

**G.H.**  What was inspiring for us (Hard Werken) came out of art and music, and theatre.

**A.B.***  There were a few good designers and we whispered their names…Now everything is design, and you see that the most important client in the Netherlands, KPN [post and telecommunications holding], who set the tone, has completely changed. I'm working now on the annual report and it has to look like the annual report of the Albert Heijn (Ahold) [supermarket chain]. They asked me, but Gerard would have done the same job. It's all Joop van den Ende [media entertainment corporation].

Things changed very fast. What we now have looks like design, it's accepted as a form, but the content is gone.

**G.H.**  You'll find more content (strangely enough) with fast moving consumer goods like Nike, who try to set up more than just design. What I'm trying to say is that Nike works with creative designers, who deliberately introduce the unexpected. They can no longer make do with a basic managing team.

**A.B.***  The same thing happened to the PTT [now KPN]. (…) It's a huge group to work with. It's prepared by Kunst en Vormgeving ['Art and Design department']. They try to do their best, but all the managers in the KPN have other ideas. We're now at breaking point. I'm not interested in design, I'm interested in the next step, because these people, the young managers,

*for his posters, he has worked in almost every field of design. It is impossible to trace all of his activities, but maybe that is just it. As he stated himself: 'I like to move around to earn my bread'. His work has always been personal, provocative, humorous*

**and above all, has never been caught in mainstream style, even though the man himself introduced 'Generic' opposed to 'Dutch' or 'States' Design.**
**So what's the motivation, or justification for design? What about this temptation to satisfy the hungry eyes of millions who always want more? (although figures show that only 22% of the world's population has access to free-press).**
**Is it reproduction, overproduction or worthless entertainment?**

the MBA yuppies, are ruling the Netherlands.

J.B.    What Gerard says is true, designers should be able to talk about their own ideas. (...)

G.H.    You have to be able to talk their language.

D.B.    Why do people go to an MBA programme? Not because they are interested in the connection between poetry, jazz and painting, but because they want to make a lot of money before they are forty. That's a different motivation.

G.H.    I'm not sure, I think that's a big generalisation.

D.B.    It is (on purpose).

G.H.    But that is typical of the kind of stereotyping you should avoid.

A.B.    But it's the same as if you say that young designers now are just waiting around till some money falls from the sky, and that they are not going round trying to find business.

G.H.    I'm talking about one particular group of designers that I got to know in the past ten years; they were people who lived mostly on the grants of the Fonds [Foundation for fine arts, design and architecture; funding body], and these people are considered to be the finest in Holland. And they have not - yet - the faintest idea how to continue when the grant stops. So what will they do? They will probably start teaching.

F.S.    Is that really a big problem? You managed it.

G.H.    It is a question of self image. You have to work from within. There are still people who think society and business are two different things. That's a very archaic way of thinking.

F.S.    I agree you can still do both things.

A.B.*    Talking about the future, we designers have to assume the role of communication artists, because the clients are fed up with advertising agencies, they don't have ideas. We do, but our attitude has to change. It doesn't matter if you make a poster for James Lee Byars, Nike or Bijenkorf [department store]. It all comes to the same thing.
You can say, well, I don't want to work with a certain kind of product, that's up to you, but I think it's all the same (as far as the form is concerned). But for example KPN, the people who spoke to me five years ago, in some respects tell a completely different story now. It's theatre, and I like it. Every step we take is checked by a group of lawyers in New York. What they say goes. That has never happened before in my life. This is a new time.

G.H.    That's also because they want to get into the stock exchange.

A.B.*    It ends up as form. It's not only the fault of the designers.(...)

G.H.    It is interesting, if you go to the Stedelijk, you'll find that - up to 1965 - there is actually a lot of commercial stuff in the archives. For some reason, after 1967, no good commercial stuff was created, according to the curator. So you can see a certain break in time. That was the moment when graphic design came of age, so to speak, through Wim Crouwel, and you had the difference between high and low culture. But if you look at the TD [Total Design] book of 10 years ago, you can see commercial work by Anthon. It is a matter of information.

G.H.    Back to strategies. When I wanted to make a Sinterklaaslijstje [list with what you want from Santa Claus], I thought about what we want, rather than what clients expect from us.

D.B.    What do they expect?

G.H.    That it works, but that's tough, because it's an ephemeral business, and there are no reliable ways to test effectiveness.(...) You have to make your own priorities.

D.B.    The task is to represent your own time, you're offering a piece of contemporary time, is that it?

G.H.    It is more that designers are media animals, they can plug their clients into the media world. That which is outside in the world, most of what is perceived, is not design, that's make-up. You cannot just look at MTV and say that is design, you need a certain awareness for that, which most people don't have.

D.B.    How interested are designers in the public's view?

A.B.*    We are not product designers, it's too complicated to test the results of our work. (...) I'm a craftsman.

D.B.    How about the discrepancy between the way people see you and how you see yourself?

A.B.* First, the way you look at yourself; I make commercial things, and in my free time nice things, and that will never stop. I do my job, and I have the luck to meet interesting clients (for example Gerard Jan Reijnders - Toneelgroep Amsterdam).

G.H. I do have the problem that I grew up as a fine artist, making work within undefined borders. (...) If you look at the heritage of that period, you can call it site-specific art. A designer is working as a craftsman and a thinker, so he's in the best position. If you get dissatisfied with your work you have to take the initiative, that's when you can change from within. The MBA values are being eroded, and that's where you have to jump in, not like the artist with his beret and palette, but with a true understanding of what people are about. You have to create a platform for yourself, be your own client, or use the project subsidy of the Kunstenfonds [Foundation for the arts].

A.B.* I got that money once for the Artist Studio project, but then there was a big problem, because I came up with an art product, and the others were designers.

S.B. There are also people in the system who don't have both qualities.

G.H. That's why I say people should -if they start for themselves- structure it, find a partner and then go to the Fonds and produce a magazine in one year time.

S.B. But once you start, you find out very quickly that this is the way it works. You have this idea, find the people and then you ask for the money. You have all this energy before you start, you cannot plan it.

G.H. There is a strong culture of intuition in the Dutch art schools, it's a bit of a problem!

X.X. A beautiful problem!

R.T. It's a bit of a problem, in that it is an escape from accountability.

G.H. But if you find out, where are you going to find the tools?

K.M. These are young people. When I hear you, as a young designer you were motivated on a completely different level then you're now imposing...

G.H. Now I'm going to say something terrible. When I was 25 or 28 I would never have gone

## Answering with creativity and imagination is not enough, you have to raise questions wi

F.S. Do you see the Fonds as a client? That they can demand something?

G.H. Well, funding is always a disaster, but the applications are also appalling. The language, structure, presentation and thinking (especially). It's much more simple than that. The thesis culture is very limited, everybody should read Umberto Eco's 'How to write a thesis'. A classic.

S.B. In every profession you have a few very abusive persons, and a lot of people under them. You make it sound so **negative**. You talk about the few people who have the qualities to survive.

G.H. It has to do with culture. The problem is me. That's what's negative. You can be an incredibly talented visual producer, who has a lot of interesting ideas but who perhaps can't think very constructively in a way that expresses them clearly. If you lose out to somebody who has no imagination (but has an excellent way of writing a thesis), it's a pity.

out forcing revolutionary ideologies. This hidden agenda is not very popular and perceived as 'Don Quixote-like', but a product or message should ask if it helps to be of importance for a sustainable environment or surroundi. Does it save or produce energy or action, doe it make a statement about the current situation? Maybe graphic design is not the right tool to accomplish these things. Some see this as an archaic way of thinking, we are no longer in the Seventies, we are dealing with different, more realistic picture where privatisation and globalisation rule the market and force us to make adjustments to, or falsifications of your original creative idea. Experienced designers will tell you that it's all play-acting, it doesn't matter who you work for, Greenpeace and Nike are both on t side of the powers that be. It's nice to have utopian views, but history has shown that revolutionary figures always end up on the

to a post-graduate course, I would never have actually sat down, for 4 hours, and listened to two old farts talking about how the future is unrolling. Everybody needs his dose of stupidity, otherwise you never get ahead in the world. But there are limits.

K.M.    I completely agree, but right now I believe, more or less, in the art of design. It's the most important art of them all. And now I get the idea that the problematic side is getting out of proportion.

G.H.    I don't think you can do without intuition. You either have to find a partner, who can draw up a structure or strategy, or do it yourself. Otherwise you'll get isolated, that's the worst thing that can happen to a designer. Then you have to design your own milk cartons and paste them onto the milk cartons you buy, a terrible prospect.

K.M.    In the 60's you started by yourselves, with friends. There was no Fonds.

A.B.*    You can do that now. A few years ago I started a new magazine in the same way as Hitweek [pop music magazine/ed.], without a penny, we found the money to print it, made a deal with the distributor, and he printed it, we didn't know what happened, sometimes he gave money. Everybody is working for free, including famous photographers, because they know it will be printed very well so it's also for their portfolio. A lot of energy goes into it, we like doing it, nobody is asking for it.

P.H.    But it's different from Hitweek.

A.B.*    The context is completely different.

G.H.    He has enough records.

A.B.*    My house is full of records. At the moment there are a lot of projects on the market, and only a few forecasting agencies. Our forecasting always looks two years ahead. The organisation has to produce advertising ideas for their own products and introduce them to the buyer's market. In this way they can find out what will be successful and then they can produce for the real market. During our first year, we produced a magazine - these 'books' cost 5000 guilders, or more when you ask the studio to make an estimate. There's a group of cooks, chefs, graphic designers, textile/fashion designers who need a magazine like that. It's not a big group but it's nice to work with them on this, that's the only reason why I do it. I pay myself for having fun.

D.B.    Do you have to prove that you both are different?

G.H.    In the 70's, Anthon was the only designer that I really knew out of all of them, because I really didn't care a shit what Jan or Wim did, for me that was just old men's stuff. His work had to do with mass-pop-culture, and the work of the other two was about design itself. Their discussions about form were appreciated much more at the Rietveld [art academy]. We were in a vacuum and we had to take our sources from elsewhere.

D.B.    You have said something like 'I'm on my fifth cycle of loving and hating Crouwel's work; this is the way thinking develops, it's not a linear process, its a cyclical one'.

G.H.    It's cyclical in that you keep going over the same ground, but what's not cyclical is the fact that you're constantly changing and learning.

A.B.*    I know the feeling. You know that something is high quality when, even though sometimes it seems superficial, it hits the nail right on the head. Exactly. He was important, as a stylist; people before him, like Dick Elffers, were not graphic designers at all.

G.H.    But he started out like that. In a talkshow with him, I said that I thought it was a pity that he became so structuralistic, that that's why a lot of beautiful things are not made any more. One could say that a lot of things in the 50's were very subjective, and he made his choice. But there's something else; as far as I

one of the formerly despised king. So, is ere a code book for the designer, or is ere no room for ethical or humanistic nsiderations?

t if a code book ends up being a political rality or subjective generalisation, but could address some points about shar-, being both consumer and maker, and a appreciation of nature. Beeke's latest ssion has nothing to do with coat-hang-, Shaker-design or Inuit-igloo building, a collaboration with Lidewij Edelkoort, vis Shah and others, to produce, edit d distribute the View on Colour maga-

zines / books (together with

59

know, Total Design was not founded by Wim Crouwel, but by the Schwartz brothers, and they were imitating a well known structure from abroad.

D.B.    It was based on the British model.

G.H.    So, graphic design in Holland started with business partners, that's my point.

K.M.    You also mentioned before that Crouwel was a manager in his profession. A lot of people were working for him.

A.B.*    That reflects what I said in the beginning, that I'm not satisfied with only working in the studio, because of the effect on quality. Wim and I had a lot of discussions, I wanted to change the name of the studio to Pentagram. He said: 'Dear little Anthon, they are stars, and we are not stars.' 'Come on,' I said 'You are a **star**!' 'No,' he replied, 'I don't want to be a star, I would like to work on the second rung, and let all these freelancers jump over us and fall down.' I said: 'We won't fall down, we are working in heaven!' He answered: 'The best studio in the Netherlands is BRS; they are not creative at all, but they work on a certain level, and all these clients like their work, there's no risk, it is well done, and done in time.'

K.M.    He was the first who realised that the two together is good design.

G.H.    No, what he did was turn his design into bookkeeping, and so he conserved a lot of energy, and he wanted to be second-best, from what I heard. It doesn't have to be like that, but for him that was the embodiment of functionalism. In the 80's we were producing a nightly paper for the Rotterdam Film Festival, everybody was having a good time. Crouwel came in, looked at the photographs, checked the measurements on his calculator, gave instructions and went away. What this expressed to me, was that he didn't have to deal with all the fuzzy stuff. (...) Karel, it doesn't have to mean that everybody has to become a manager, but most artists know about power structures and we don't. I still think this gets too little attention.

K.M.    I still have the fear that commercial knowledge will become the most important asset.

G.H.    Sure, most good designers are born as free artists, but still, most of them had a traditional education; they know how to think. It only

Poster
'Aids, the killing bite of love'
World Aids Day
Items 5/6, 1993

takes five minutes to learn about marketing. It's all about education, there are ways of doing things, but you are subject to strict rules and you have to know how to sustain yourself.

D.B.    Yes, it's a tight structure, but what about relying on your own initiative?

G.H.    If you're from the right family, you can cope, but otherwise..., the art schools are separate from all other kinds of education.

N.B.    I somehow have the feeling, that with all this marketing ideas we are narrowing our field. If you promote all of this, we will have too many designers.

A.B.*    There are too many already, and they're not all good. So if you're working in education you have to aim for the middle level. Give them the right tools; the lower level will fall away and the highest will survive by itself. The clients I was working for in the beginning didn't know anything, now they're all trained.

K.M.    Yes, but the clients of this generation are completely different.

A.B.*    I don't agree, I see a lot of simulations, the yuppies are around. Business has become structured. It's like Shakespeare for me! But if as a young designer you were to think, 'I want to do this annual report', he or she would be in a mental hospital in two days. It's impossible.

A.B.* + G.H.    

# Amsterdam C.S. -

## Eindhoven,

Niels Biersteker, vier april negentienzesennegentig

# int er vie wi ng A. B. *

*Magazine spread*
*View on Colour*
*I.D. march/april, 1996*

RECOVERY

No, I quit(...)
I had a lot of publicity, I am a sort of publicity magnet; radio, television and the press always come to me to ask me if it is all right, and Wim has always had publicity, but the rest of the people, Jolijn van der Wouw, Ben Bos, Paul Mijksenaar, they were very serious... And of course that created bad feeling, because they dealt with all the clients that Crouwel had put to one side, and who were generating a lot of money by that time. They were making the money for the bureau. Wim Crouwel was the flag and I was the drum, the disturbing element, and at a certain point that started to create tension. They were making much more money and were doing much more work. I had a lot more publicity, invitations and prizes. That did not really work and Ben Bos especially was very annoyed by it; he did not think it was the right balance. So I simply had to go. My idea that I could shape the bureau according to my ideas, the way I thought it should be, did not work at all. I am not a Wim Crouwel, he can do that. It is a question of organisation and having a plan, whilst I am much more about making, on my own. I am much more - I don't mean it in the way this sounds - an artist than Wim Crouwel, who is much more of an organiser. But anyway, at that point I quit and started again on my own.

terior View). If you're not able to
y this item, it's best to read the
ticle by Rick Poynor. To make col-
:tor items instead of overproduced
sposables seems to be a legitimate
int of departure, and by creating
ends or bending them at a certain moment in time, it looks as if it's possible to have an

*Together you had a sort of image, an aura of 'we will get you the product, you can depend on that', whilst with you - I can imagine - they had more the feeling of 'there's that clown again' or however you want to put it; we never know where we are at.*

I am not a clown at all. No, I liked to disturb the idea of what they expected of TD and also about how time was shaped. That order is still there of course, but at that time the clients were the first generation of businesses coming out of the war. Before that there was absolutely nothing, well yes, Boffie coffee, and Van Houten, but those businesses grew, and thank God TD was there to make it all, and sub-bureaux were set up, such as BRS; they turned it into an organisation. Gert Dumbar and I - we are from the same generation - did not want that; we wanted

61

*this magazine*

*AB: " You don't*

*money. You*

Magazine spread
View on Colour
I.D. march/april, 1996

*a colour, when you change, the colour changes. It is very delicate.'*

to disturb all that. We felt like tralala. Then culture started to emerge. It was already there of course but it was hyped enormously; another theatre, another museum, more of this and more of that. The Sixties had a great influence on Gert and me. Gert can really turn highly organised companies upside down; all the house styles he creates, you cannot believe that a serious business wants to work with that. I think that it is very temporary. At a time like that a director's son thinks 'I have to have that', but the next generation of management does not want anything to do with it; they want it to look good again but they will ditch the tralala. But that has had its function too; you cannot go on shocking for ever. At a certain point it is over. You think, 'Okay, stop walking into rooms with your pants down.' You must not overdo it. I have done that too. In the Sixties, we were busy really shocking people, with images on the streets that had never been seen before. Those sort of images become the norm and cease to shock anybody. That has been taken over by the Tros, Veronica [broadcasting organisations] and all the shit that's around at the moment. They think 'let's take that,' I mean, you can't turn on the television without finding a sex programme where a girl utters a soft h. It has not got quality anymore; it has become rubbish. But that did not exist before; the erotic world was still a hidden, mysterious one. Now it has become an enormous industry, completely uninteresting, unless you go and sit with those sort of images amongst things that have not been touched yet. Not that I am still doing that; that period is over.

***Are there any possibilities left to slip through all that?***

No, but it is no longer necessary. My provocation is almost that I work in the Crouwel school way again, that I make the horizontal vertical. So that a great tranquillity is created - content, not form. With Gert Dumbar it is still as if you are at a funfair; he is still working with the wealth and excesses of form, but actually nobody is interested in that any more. Now everybody wants to read again, to be well-informed. But what is the quality of that information. That is what I am concerned with - to provoke Dutch design. Because everything is possible in it, all those little Americans, French and

effect on patterns of consumption. But of course the future can't be predicted and the images and language taken from the present are merely a selection of those in existence. Maybe I am looking too hard for valid motives, but if it were possible to change human behaviour or to reflect it in order to change it, this magazine might be on the right track. By dramatising contemporary life-style, seducing, and posing as a fairy-tale like forest (where the wedding of David Copperfield and

*money. you do*

*fun. What I*

Germans come here and think: 'Well, in Holland you can do what you like, all sorts of things are happening there!' Well, that is over; nobody wants that any longer; one frill cannot compete with another. So you need information again, tranquillity. After that there will be a generation again, maybe it is you, which says: 'We will beat the drum again,' but that is the rhythm of society, always.

*What you are saying, that started maybe five years ago, the return to simplicity, to sobriety of style.*

Yes, I introduced that more or less with View on Colours. I call it 'Generic design' (Gert calls it 'States design'); coming from the genes. So it starts, a new wave. But the clients - you must not lose sight of them - they are really only now ready for the frills and the excesses. They think: 'My neighbour, uncle or second cousin has got that too and they are doing all right, aren't they?'

*The neighbour's grass is always greener?*

Not that. Look, most designers have one generation of clients. Most have only one generation, they educate them, they learn from it, are chastened by it,

Claudia Schiffer could take place), is an exaggeration in order to ridicule. Beeke likes to see graphic design as a tool of social criticism, in a period where computer-based 'rococo' has fuelled his extravagance. To offer the audience a way into democratic discussion is important, but also raises questions about the use of fashion in this as with the skin-deep features of Toscani's children, who gave birth to other green-labelled lifeforms. The marketing of a global consciousness is widely discussed, and I don't think Beeke and Edelkoort are heading in the direction of the aforementioned magazine

buy their second home in France out of it, and then a new generation of designers comes along and pushes them to one side, but they still have the old clients to fall back on. They don't interest me. I am much more interested in the young generation, they keep me awake.

*But to my mind the conversation at the Jan van Eyck Akademie was rather pessimistic in the sense that the new generation of clients are people who fly over from America and decree: 'yes, that is how it will be done, no, this is how it must be done.'*

I don't know if I would put it that way, but rather in the sense - I think - that a lot is missing from management courses. The whole of management is geared towards how to keep control, how to deal with your workforce, how to get clients, but the publicity side...in the old days Mr. van Houten or Mr. Ford did that himself. We aren't all geniuses like that but you should have some idea of how you want to present a product on the market.

*Covers View on Colour*

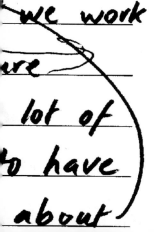

So I think that a large chunk of education has to be introduced into higher management courses; communication techniques. Not just about advertising, but also from an aesthetic and philosophical viewpoint: 'what are we doing?' - the dressing up of a company, somebody else does the selling, we are the cooks, the dressmakers.

*But would you say that it is also the other way round, that the people at art school should learn more about communication techniques?*
Yes, that is also happening, and it must. The situation as it is at the moment, that another year has been taken off, down to four years, that is absolutely shameless. It is happening at the universities too. I believe that you now have to do your BA [in Dutch: 'Dr'] in three years; well I don't know that I want to go to a doctor like that with my gallstones. It can hardly be done. Even if you could pack all the information into such a short period, it also has to be digested. You have to be able to shit it out too at some point; it simply needs time. But I am sure that it is true that the programmes become more dense, with more information, that it is all becoming more serious.

*Are you still active in education yourself?*
No, but I will probably go back to Eindhoven, and I give guest lectures in America, but that does not amount to much, it is not really teaching. You do that for six weeks, now and then. But I will probably teach at the communications department again in Eindhoven. I have done that for a while, Guus Ros is doing it at the moment, but we will probably swap again. I am rather looking forward to that; I now have much clearer ideas than before, about what vitamins you need on your plate as a student to become healthy and stay that way.

*In France you have one of those elite schools. Eighty percent of present politicians attended it; very analytical, rather pessimistic.*
I think, if that is the case, it is bad for the market as well as for the students. There are very few really good students. There are not many people who can really map out their own route, who can invent their own life. Most people have to be guided, not everybody is a Pasteur. You don't become one, you are one. The rest have to be given guidance.

(*Colours* by Toscani), but I can see something controversial in the audience they have chosen (textile/ clothing designers, car designers and colour/style consultants). I hope they will also agree that 'enough is enough', and realise that we don't need most of their colourful make-up. Of course,

*A.Beeke with K.Schippers*
*Documentaires over grafische*
*vormgeving; no. 9, 1979*

'La poire d'Erik Satie'. Daarom had ik een mandje met in vloeipapier verpakte peren voor **hem** meegebracht. **Hij** zette de mand op een lage tafel en zei: 'It's a better decoration than flowers'. En ook: 'Satie should have been around'. Mocht ik die woorden CITEREN**?** Ja, maar dan wel **GROOT** of klein; **hij** had altijd

*Poster*
*Glück, Globe Theatre*
*Affiche; no.3/4, 1994*

Of course there has to be space for the individual in that, but not like the apathetic period of the Sixties and Seventies, where everything was possible; that sort of education did not have any structure. That is how I see it, although the weaker ones have to be supported.

*I read recently a report, by the Ministry for Economic Affairs, about telecommunications, globalisation and privatisation; you name it, the weakest are being ploughed under.*
But that has always been the case; a baker who bakes

bread that hasn't been cooked properly stands little chance (although there are customers who do not know what bread should taste like), but somebody who knows what good bread tastes like goes to a baker who bakes good bread. It remains like that of course, it never rises.

*But, when I look around, a feeling for romance seems to be lost a bit with all that target-thinking.*

It's up to you to give it swing, your generation has

**people do tend to buy useless gadgets, beautiful and expensive clothes and look for**

to do that. The sentimental feeling of the fin de siècle, of the year 2000, that there is nothing after that any more, that by then we will have had everything; well, I don't know, the moon will just rise again, it will be Wednesday again, you have to pay the rent. It doesn't change a fuck, but you will have arrived in a new era. I mean, if I were to produce a book now and it would come out in 1999, I would rather have it come out in 2000; the other book would be a book of the last century, an old-fashioned book. I think that feeling is stimulating. You saw the same in the change from the 19th to the 20th century; Jugendstil, Art Deco, an amazing number of inventions. Enough is happening, it will happen again, only we don't see it, we are farting about with the Internet. Who knows what will emerge from it, the whole studio is busy trying to get to grips with it, they only show me the little things, because they know I haven't a clue where the buttons are. I don't have to do that any more; you have to do that, I can only look to see whether there is content, form.

*What are the other projects which you put all your energy into?*

I am busy with a few books, finishing some posters, doing some artwork for myself (all those studios, all those artists), and I would like to make another magazine, an erotic magazine, along the lines of View on Colours, not a sex magazine. Apart from that I would like, as I said, to immerse myself more in education. I just happen to be working in a very broad field.(...) Then I have got links with some South American countries, to teach at some colleges and give workshops, because that is very important there. It is a continent that is so rich and so poor, which lacks so much information, all those papers we read, and that they don't. The kids at those schools, they don't actually know what they are doing; they are still processing the legacy of the Sixties. Even the teachers, sometimes they get a magazine from Europe or America and they think, 'Oh my God, all the door-knobs must be like that - yellow with a blue dot!' All imitation culture. zI always say: 'Kids, in the 16th century we started book printing in Holland.' We were the first country which industrialised the invention. In the rest of Europe they were against it, only here we thought, 'we can make money with this.' The others thought: 'No, an invention of the devil, handwriting is much more beautiful.' You come across the same conservatism all the time, in every business. A new machine means: five men without work or five men working in the garden. There are always victims but the next generation gets over it. Anyway, in Holland the presses were rolling, the paper churned out, but do you necessarily have to do the same thing in Lima suddenly? Do they need that? I wouldn't know but they aren't looking for it. Everywhere there are imitation Elvis Presleys walking around while they have their own Elvis, only he looks different. You have to talk about that with teachers and students, so that they look at what sort of shit they are standing in and what fruit it is bearing. How fertile the shit is. Believe me, it is a very interesting subject!

*Yeah, yeah. Recently Chris Vermaas was giving a talk at the Academy in The Hague and he waxed lyrical about the lack of development there (Mexico) and what they were getting out of it.*

Naturally, we like that, but it is not enough for them. When I used to visit Poland I wanted to print my posters on Polish paper, but you could not get it anywhere; they were ashamed of it. Of course it was shit; you could see straight through it. But I wanted it. We made many attempts - with Tomaszewski and Swierzy - to get into a printing factory, but they thought; 'A designer from the West, he immediately thinks that..., so we won't.' And now Poland is free, or rather, you can drive in and out of it, but it is being governed by the mafia. The whole poster culture has gone, it has all become polished.

*You often talk about helping one another for free. Is that something you miss?*

We do many things for free, because there are people who haven't got any money, but we don't really do it for free. I give it as a present, so that nobody thinks: 'Oh well, I got it for free!' no, you get it as a present; it does not have any value when it is free. If you get it as a present you can't carry on asking: 'Can I have another present?' It is a different attitude.

Exactly. Then you have to think of something else again. And so I am not going to go into other fields which I know nothing about (Internet). But maybe later I will, when I understand how it works; not the technique, but the creation. When Renë Knip says: 'What typeface is that?' then I think, 'How should I know, 'I choose intuitively. In the past I used to know, now there are hundreds of thousands of typefaces.

*But you don't feel the need to let the sort of time you are living in speak through your work?*

Yes of course, but View on Colour is just that. If in a hundred years time you look back at this period, people might well laugh themselves silly about that magazine, but come what may, it will emerge as something which helped to shape our time.

*Maybe that is what's most beautiful, when people can laugh about it...*

That is the most beautiful. At some point I took part in an exhibition in Brussels, Europalia. Every year Belgium chooses a country and lets it show its cultural high points. Wim Schippers was exhibiting as well and people could not stop

the most successful image, but the point of the criticism might be lost if you depend on

*Many designers feel a need to bring an underlying theory or business philosophy to the fore. Discussions and interviews, that is what graphic design should be in Holland.*

As I already said, I am looking for an incredible simplification which will work as a sort of tranquillity. The statement I am making with our magazine resurfaces in my other work, but I am not going to say how things should be. And I do not want a big studio with 40 staff either. I'll only live a short time, later does not exist, you can only do it now, by starting today; only the kicks matter. Some people need a needle or a pill for it; I have got a little magazine; just as expensive, just as addictive. You have to fill out your own life, with your talent; I have not got that much talent really, but I have a lot of energy, and the good luck that some people saw something in me.

*And the best thing is that everything will end up on the rubbish heap in a few years, all those covers...*

laughing; they really were wetting themselves; the best compliment you can get. The best thing is to be Stan Laurel or Oliver Hardy, isn't it?

*No theory can match that.*

Exactly. Nobody can match that.

*I actually think this is rather a nice END.*

Well, yes?

*Or have you still got a message for the boys and girls of the next generation?*

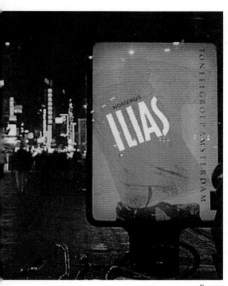

*Poster*
*Ilias, Toneelgroep Amsterdam*
*Items; no.8, 1994*

such an audience. I'm sure View on Colour wants to convey a massage, but doesn't believe in radical change, and the 'happy few' feeling is still present. The lay-out of the pages is - to my taste - sometimes too literally related to high functionalism, and is holding back expressional potential, by keeping text and image too separate. I miss the playfulness and 'feeling of fun' that I see in Beeke's other work. This assertion of high functionalism is good, but I do hope it grabs the attention of his audience, rather than limiting design, because I still believe that creative energy cannot be fitted into a Crouwel-like uniform. Only time will tell whether people will respond to the suggestions that we should be satisfied with less, live

Oh no, they will have to find out for themselves. I am not a moralist.

*Or a cynic?*
No, I am not an -ist or an -ic. I do my own thing, I always admire those who do not abuse others.

*Are there people in Holland who you would say, 'They should be treated better? '*
Yes certainly. For instance, it makes me sick when I see a bunch of kids (squatters) who get into an empty bank. They have to leave and then they turn on all the taps. Who do they think they are getting at with that? Those kids should really go to an education camp! The building can't help it that it is empty, it is a piece of culture, a beautiful building. Why do a bunch of wet-behind-the-ears kids have to do that? I think it is scandalous, that is about nothing, like pissing through somebody's letterbox. Ridiculous.

*On the other hand, imagine it isn't 'piss artists' but a group of homeless who get into a building like that. That is the other side of the coin of course.*
There have been very good actions in the past, I am not talking about that, about 'political correctness'. But that building - which isn't a building to live in - is just empty for a little while, until it acquires another function, but is a beautiful building - beautiful floors, ceilings, walls, the 17th century at its best. Then you get a group of those mohicans and they turn on all the taps. Well, what fun. That is just a small example; there are more. Such things happen in government too, so that you think: 'How dare they?' The whole drugs mess which at the moment...

*What mess?*
The drug trafficking situation, that has been an incredible abuse, of people who have sworn an oath to always stick to the law. But again, I will not shout it from the rooftops, nobody is interested in that. I am not a public figure, but it does bother me, there are no norms. Even the minister says: 'I drove 80 mph;' she can drive 125 as far as I am concerned, I do that too now and then - as a manner of speaking - but she has to drive at 60 or 70, even if she says 'I was in a hurry.' We all drive fast because we are in a hurry.

67

**Yes, everybody is in a hurry.**

I understand it all, but recently I got a fine because I drove at 31. What a lot of wankers. I am actually a minister too, am I not? But anyway, it has always been like that; it does not bother me, but norms of politeness have disappeared. Few people are just polite to one another, out of kindness.

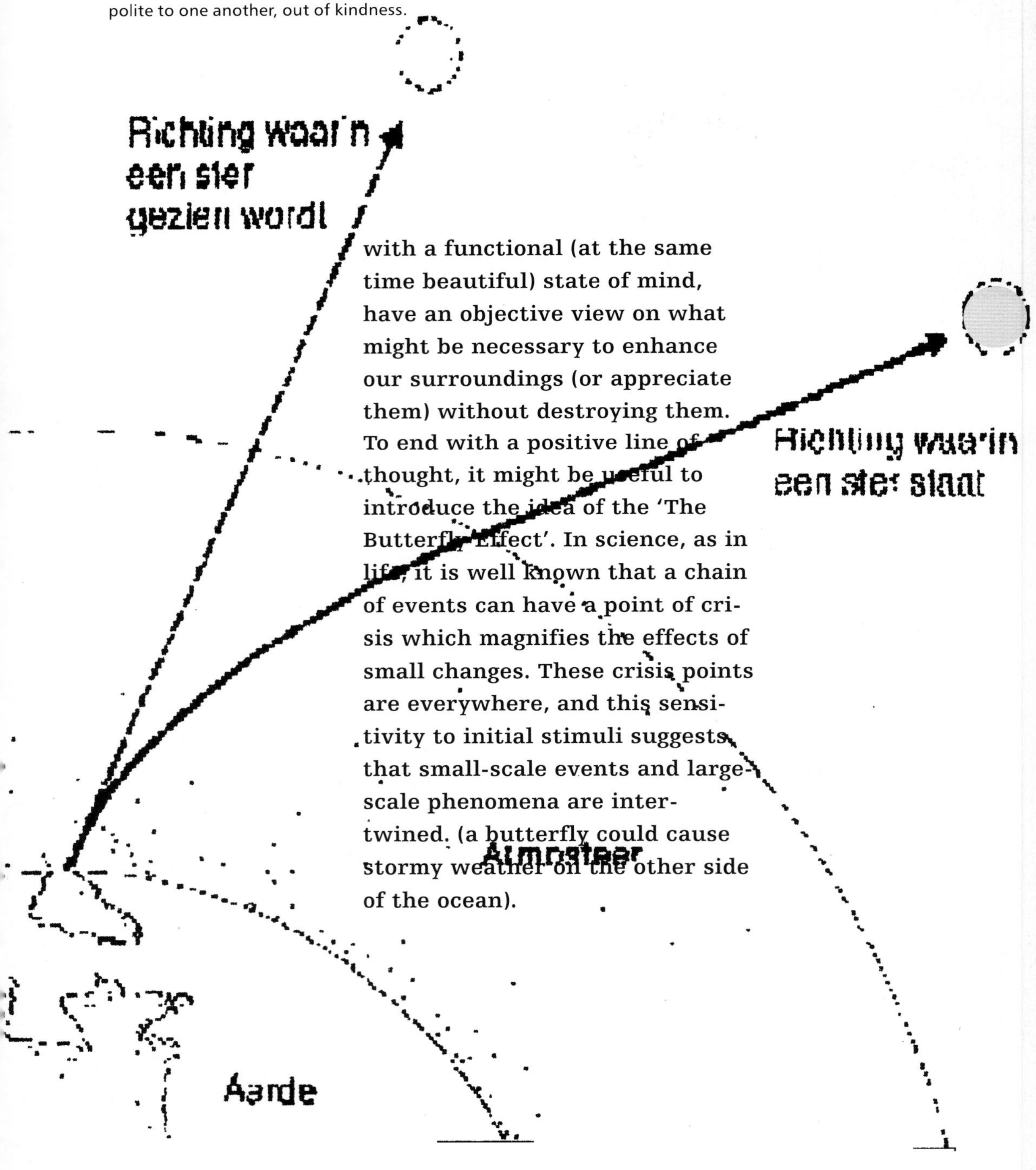

Richting waar'n
een ster
gezien wordt

with a functional (at the same time beautiful) state of mind, have an objective view on what might be necessary to enhance our surroundings (or appreciate them) without destroying them. To end with a positive line of thought, it might be useful to introduce the idea of the 'The Butterfly Effect'. In science, as in life, it is well known that a chain of events can have a point of crisis which magnifies the effects of small changes. These crisis points are everywhere, and this sensitivity to initial stimuli suggests that small-scale events and large-scale phenomena are intertwined. (a butterfly could cause stormy weather on the other side of the ocean).

Richting waar'n
een ster staat

Atmosfeer

Aarde

Lars Heller
<u>Unknown gangster</u>

Gerard Hadders

'THIS THING IS BIGGER THAN ALL OF US, BABY.'
—*UNKNOWN GANGSTER*—

ART

4

'Oliviero Toscani has just published a book which starts with a kind of offensive against the advertising industry. He talks about the waste of huge sums of money, the social uselessness of commercial communication, lies, secret temptation, racism, crimes against intelligence, individual peace, language and creativity. What is your position towards this account of daily practice in the advertising industry?'

'Do you have information as to whether it is successful?'

'I would say that Toscani makes very good advertising. It's a little bit hypocritical coming from him. What he means is interesting of course, but at the same time you can't generalise about advertising. What Toscani means particularly has to do with the global advertising culture and with the most strongly developed aspects of advertising. Advertising — as far as I know — may be a waste of money. Toscani's own work is in a way a waste of money.'

'Yesterday I read that there is a guy in Dunkerque in France who is suing Benetton over the fact that two of the shops in Dunkerque have filed for bankruptcy. The bankruptcy had to do with Toscani's advertising campaign, so that guy says that Benetton put him out of business through this advertising.

That's an angle on it. There is something you can call the added value of product advertisement and then you have illusionism. Every advertisement is illusionist. A lot of people knock advertising in general, but it's not so much the thinking behind advertising that bothers me, because that comes from the mind of creative people like you and me — they can be pretty stupid, pretty bright or pretty sick. My problem lies much more in the aspects of distribution that we know and that we see. Advertising is one thing, while its diffusion and abuse is another. It is more and more difficult these days to avoid advertising. In a place where I used to be able to see a nice view of meadows with cows somewhere to the north of this town I now have to look at three hearts by Toscani (which is one of his worst posters). It is not Toscani's fault, nor is it the fault of those producing advertising, or the fault of the illusionist aspects of advertising, that this billboard is there. The billboard is there for economic reasons to do with the increasing infiltration of advertising. I once took an interesting photograph on this subject. I was in the south of India and there was a very badly rubbled wall on which was painted an advertisement for Coca-Cola. The instrumentality is

'OK, but I want to talk more about the mechanisms of advertising. Toscani for example believes that a big enterprise like Fiat, which now builds quite good cars, has a bad image because their advertising has not changed in years; it always shows a sexy Italian girl next to a shiny car and that does nothing to help change their image. He thinks that if an enterprise starts some kind of social communication, for instance Fiat communicating about drug addiction, that would improve the reputation of the company.'

'What about public opinion towards advertising? Has that changed? Has consumerism become more careful, do people see that resources get wasted?'

really the big problem; take for instance the fact that the commercial television-stations in Holland now want the Dutch government to ban the BBC from the Dutch cable network because it is not functional in the way they consider television to be functional.'

'If you want to attack the illusionist aspects of advertising then you have to say that Fiat must provide product information and leave it at that. It is ridiculous that one private company's creative director should demand from another private company's creative director that he does the same thing. Fiat has to sell cars and Fiat has to donate money to the Italian state - which is of course always a complete waste (laughs) — and fund an independent foundation. It is ridiculous to suppose that a private company — and particularly a private company as wealthy and influential as the Andreotti-family — should want to inform the people about certain things which are actually the responsibility of the state.'

'The problem is that fifteen years ago the question was: Is advertising irritating or not? Nowadays the question is: Are particular advertisements irritating or not? When the so-called generation X (which stands for exciting, I guess) talks about advertising and knocks advertising they don't mean advertising in general but the advertising they consider to be stupid. That usually means advertising which is not directed at them.

The audience is much more aware of advertisements in general, but is much less aware of what advertising really is because they have become completely surrounded by commercial publications. So advertising is now their landscape. You can't expect a twenty year old to imagine a world without advertising. It's gone so far that if you look at culture and the bearers of culture you couldn't imagine a western culture without advertising, it has actually become part of our heritage and part of our life. Our language would probably be different, our way of looking at things would be different, etc. without advertising. There are differences between one country and another. These differences are apparent in an

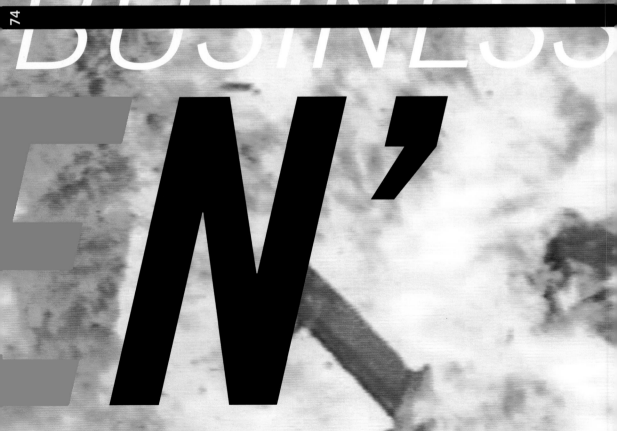

audience's mental attitude towards advertising. For example the illusionist approach is nowhere as well developed as it is in England, and the illusionist approach is particularly well developed around products that have extreme limitations on how they can be advertised, for instance, cigarettes: five years ago, ten years ago, you could still advertise cigarettes in connection with sports and pleasure. In America and in England this was completely forbidden and they had to advertise cigarettes without even portraying people. That has led to the most stunning, interesting pieces of visual heritage from advertising. In a way, these are much more interesting than the things Toscani has done. If there is one country in the world where commercial communication at its best can account for the best episodes in advertisements, commercial communication or graphic design - like the period of Cassandra in French design of the 20's - you could easily say it was in England in the 70's and 80's. This is how limited it is.'

'Does advertising have to change to continue to succeed in the future?'

'No, what might change is that you get a different use of telemedia, such as television. If you get developments that further individualise these media, the street will become even more important, which means that you will have commercial messages in the street even more than you have now. Look at some of the more visionary architects of our time, like Koolhaas and Jean Nouvel, and you will see that they have already designed buildings which have electronic velums, screens which can be used for projection and perhaps film.'

'In lectures, you emphasise the relevance of marketing strategies and advertising skills for the graphic designer. You place these above the intuitional creativity which is in my eyes the main tool of graphic design.'

'I think it is a tool, and it is the origin for many people, but I think you have to understand the medium in which you operate. If you were a graphic designer twenty years ago, you had to choose, more or less, between making posters and books, or making posters and making newspapers when you started your career.'

'You can make both.'

'Well if you look at the history of the industry you will see that only a few people can really

BUSINESS

EN'

do both. I'm not talking about the best examples, but if you take someone like Anthon Beeke for instance; he's a much better poster designer, and he could never do a book without the professional help of someone else – it's not his strong point. He can think about magazines and he can develop them but his main interest is the visual aspect. Anthon would never have started out as a book typographer.

There is a distinction between typography on the one hand, and the image and the visuals on the other. You choose one of these in which to specialise. I know some very fine book typographers who are working at a very high level, but if you ask them to design a poster, they are lost. If you ask an advertising person to design a book you generally get something grotesque. As a typographer your job has to be the organisation and the aesthetics of the reading material. If you design posters – I'm talking about a basic notion from a long time ago – then you will have a different orientation, an orientation towards the image, and visual constructions. Twenty or thirty years ago you had the rise of television in Holland. There were very interesting designers already working for television at that time. But it was a very limited field; I'm talking here about the Dutch situation. Now things are much more complicated. If you look at all the media you can work in, it is very important – apart from your personal orientation, your philosophy, your history, and your own creative development – to understand the field in which you are working, otherwise it is completely senseless and useless.'

'Sure, you have to be able to perform in your own medium.'

'You can perform in your medium if you understand it, I don't think anyone would disagree with that. If you are working in the visual world you have to develop yourself. To be able to operate properly in the field you have chosen, you have to understand these aspects.'

'And what about market mechanisms?'

'You don't have to absorb them, you don't have to become a real thinker like that, but what you do have to understand is the field you are working in. As far as I know, no client is going to spend money until they have a target in mind, and that's the point at which they are going to start working with you, or with somebody else. And if you don't know what they are talking about, they won't start working with you. They will work with someone they can talk to. It may be that you are a very interesting graphic designer but you are one of those mysterious artists that no one has ever heard of, although they are actually the best.'

'You have to offer the client something they don't have. Both of you have to meet on a professional platform. But you have something they want that they are not professional in.'

'No, but they are professional at what they do, otherwise, they wouldn't be in a position to be your client. So you have to be a professional too, and being professional means that you have to understand what you are doing, the field you are working in.'

'What are your strategies if you start a new job and you get a new client? What's your definition of this term 'strategy'? What are the steps you take?'

'It's basically research. Research, conclusion, concept, execution.'

'But I mean, is that new?'

'Well, research, conclusion, strategy, concept, execution, that's not new. That's what Michelangelo or Bottarotti would do.'

'Everyone wants to sell something.'

'Well, you don't always want to sell. In my experience, research and conclusion can also lead to you not taking on a job because, for instance, you're not suitable for the job, or you don't like the client. So reaching a decision could mean quite extensive research.

When I worked for the museum in Wolfsburg, I did a survey on how other museums present themselves. When I did a house style for a bank, I did a survey on how banks present themselves.'

'And what was the conclusion?'

'The conclusion is usually translated into your approach. It needs to be able to work in that field. In the case of an art museum, it must be able to compete with other museums in terms of its visual impact and you need to learn a bit about the range of possibilities in that medium. You can take it too far, but if you have no concept of what a particular museum is, what it really wants to do, and what it wants to communicate, and you start designing...
I worked with a guy on a job for the Kunstmuseum Wolfsburg. I hired him for a month so we could collaborate. On the first day he designed three logos and they were completely useless, a complete waste of time. He didn't know anything about the museum. He just started to

make logotypes. Most graphic designers just get all their mannerisms out of the cupboard; they think they have developed a style, and when they are asked they respond with the style they think they have developed themselves.'

'OK, how does your approach differ from just creating the logo along with the story?'

'What you say is incorrect, because it's not a logo with a story behind it, it's a story that has developed into a logo. That's the big difference.

You will find that it really doesn't matter whether you are designing a logo, a poster, an interface, a CD-ROM or whatever, the best route is to develop a story and then to design, not the other way round. I know it seems pretty obvious, but most designers I have met actually work the other way round. The best thing designers can learn from advertising is that nothing materialises until there is a concept.'

'That seems to me, and to you too (from what I heard in your lecture), to be a Dutch problem because there is a big distinction between advertising and graphic design here in Holland. Most of my colleagues in Germany join advertising companies after their studies.'

'Most of the graphic designers in Germany are either poster designers in the best Polish tradition who think concept is very important, or they are designers like Ott & Stein who are very formal. So formal they don't even let themselves tell a story because they say it interferes with objectivity.'

# 'IT IS ONLY SHALLOW PEOPLE WHO D BY APPEARANCES.
# THE MYSTERY OF WORLD IS THE VISIE THE INVISIBL

—*OSCAR WILDE*—

As a graphic designer I experience a personal dilemma: after ob and the dynamism residing within this profession. It seems pos work), to influence the process of change directly or indirectly an broadened: its acceptance and right to exist seem to be establis of being at a loss in a media-based world still presents more of difference between theoretical critical attempts and the practic regional action do not exclude each other in principle, but they a pressures and demands made on the design(er) lead to contrad the commercial domain of decoration and pure service.

'But their posters work pretty well don't they?'

'Yes.'

'Yeah, I saw that too. You're right.'

'Ott & Stein's?'

'But they can't make a house style, that's what I noticed.'

'If you have designed posters for five years you can of course — once you get an image and you have a continuous process going on — design a poster in an hour. I think bookcovers are a great example, because bookcovers are paying less and less. Economically speaking you can't function, you cannot make a completely original design, including buying the rights of the images, for the amount of money they will pay. That is really impossible.'

'What kind of budget are we talking about?'

'1500, ten years ago it was 1750. So now I think we actually do it for half of what we did ten years ago.'

'Can you learn marketing skills at an academy?'

'Well, marketing skills are something else. This is not about marketing skills it's about conceptuality. We were talking about knowing where and how your work functions, how to tell a story; how to get to the point where you can formulate a kind of brief for yourself in such a way that it covers your own priorities, the priorities of the client and his market. It is very important for a designer to be aware of this because otherwise they will become more and more marginalised. I see it now with computers. Computers deflate the notion of what a designer is. So now you can get yourself a designer like you order a pizza. And most people who used to be designers have now become typesetters.'

OT JUDGE

'The strange thing is: people who started like this on a PC, designing a little bit, they sell.'

'It depends on what they sell, most of the time they do not sell at the level of what you see, but they sell something you don't see, it may be that they provide a service for the client. Look at the German situation: The book is designed at the printers, individual designers that design books are very rare, but they are there and they do function. We were talking about where photography is concerned; somebody like Toscani is rare because most photographers talk a lot about content, but when they start to take photographs the content isn't there anymore.

Whatever you do as a designer, whatever direction you take, whatever the new specialism you dive into, you need to conceptualise. It's a choice I made for myself a long time ago. I still take a lot of photographs. In the early Eighties it was still a choice... I was doing three things then: I was doing autonomous work, I did graphic design and exhibition design, and I photographed. Sometimes, these three things fused together, but I decided I would never become a photographer, and I would never become an illustrator, because as a photographer or an illustrator you're working, commercially speaking, at the end of the entire process. You always have to cover up for the bad decisions made by others, and if you are a designer, and you don't acquire a position in which your concept or your way of thinking is

HE

E, NOT

tion and empiricism I recognise the potential, the opportunities
o shape life and coexistence (communication—environment—
ensitise perception. On one hand the definition of design has
connected to a demand for design. On the other hand the sense
tative question than a strongly expressed demand. The
istic circumstances remains too dominant. Global thinking and
o not complement each other in any significant way. The
s within the discourse and prompt the designer to escape into

The term 'visual communication' describes a broad field of activity. The advertising industry with its predominately commercial motivation takes up the majority of this field. Its massive presence has become an integral part of our environment. The huge budgets invested in advertising demonstrate clearly that advertising manipulates decisions and influences action and behaviour.

On the other hand conventional sounding criteria like 'target group investigation', 'remarkability', 'rating', 'promotion', 'distribution', 'edition'... embody a number of interesting

'You should at least have an orientation, an idea of how things function.'

'Those are more complex productions.'

'What do you mean?'

predominant in the production process, you will end up in the same situation where you have to cover up the fuck-ups made by people who were in the process before you.'

'I think you should have an orientation, that orientation is important for realising what things are like, so you don't create things that won't work. In the same way a director will have held a camera himself twenty years ago at the film school. I think being a director is more interesting than being a camera man. Of course, that's my own personal opinion, there are other people who would much prefer to be the camera person or to be a photographer because they want to be part of the process but they don't want to be the captain of the ship. They either cannot do it, because they don't have the necessary qualities, or they are not interested because they are more interested in certain craft aspects — as with a cameraman and the director (this comparison is not very clear, because there are very few directors who could do what a good camera and lighting person can do).'

'To devise an interface you don't have to actually create it manually. I think it can help to have some experience, but it's a complete waste of time to learn the entire production process, because we are talking about hardware; it's called software but in a way it's hardware in that it is technology, which is constantly changing. Do you want to be doing that? When you talk about interface design, you have to be careful to use the right terms. In interface design there will be different approaches depending on whether you want to design ergonomically or you want to design rhetorically. These are two completely different orientations.'

'It's tricky territory to be precise in because even when you work ergonomically you also work with rhetoric, obviously. When I use the 'wastebasket' on my Apple computer, it's a rhetorical thing. But navigating through an Apple is an ergonomic problem. If you want to make an emotional CD-ROM you are talking about a rhetorical thing that requires a different approach. I know, there's not a difference in this sense. Most people who are capable of handling the technical side of creating this stuff will not make interesting rhetorical, romantic or emotional stuff. There is no reason why this should not be the case. This is no different to the distinction between Anthon Beeke, who is the best poster designer in Holland, or Paul Mijksenaar who is the best routing designer in Holland. One has a very strong cultural interest, the other one has a very strong structural interest. I think with the new media it will be the same.'

uestions for graphic designers. To develop new realities while
hanging our environment positively, to reduce social injustice
nd the related potential for aggression, it seems to me
ssential to deal with the instrumentality of mass
ommunication in a different way.
  As designers we have to approach and use the methods of the
dvertising world to guarantee the distribution of our ideas as
vell. It is a matter of replacing a product by a meaningful
nessage. Especially given the current globalisation of
ommunication processes and the shift from national and

'Yeah, definitely. Let's go back to the influence a designer has on the identity or presentation of a big firm. How effective is that? Do they really influence decisions made in the corporate world?'

'So they became the captain of one special ship?'

'Not exactly.'

Those are the exceptions.'

Are you interested in that side?'

'I have a short story about that which answers your question. In England, in the 80's, there were graphic design companies who took communication in business, or the publicity and public relations structure, so seriously that they gradually became corporate advisors. They went from advising on communication, to advising on, for instance, the structure of corporate development.'

'Oh, they would develop from being graphic designers into being advisors on how to run a company. Some of them were so powerful they took over the financial services too. So they became bookkeepers, accountants. Of course these people were not designers, the designers were not there anymore, they took on accountants to do the accounting. The company still had the same name. I think that's the only answer you'll get. You can become as influential as you like if you master all these aspects that play a role in the entire thing. But, then of course if you do one thing, you can't do other things. If you, as a designer, become a strategic consultant the chances of you actually making the work become that much less likely. It may also be undesirable. If you are a strategic advisor on graphic communication for a client, it may be better that you're on the client's side, not on the side of the maker, because then you become a bit confused. You know what I mean?'

'Well, if the task becomes too big, you can't do both. You can't be the one who makes the product and the person who advises on it. It has to do with levels of abstraction. If you are a designer working for a company that is so big that it has a separate post for a strategic consultant then usually the number of jobs is too big for one person to handle. You will always see that a creative person becomes a strategic consultant inside a company. He will be on the client's side even inside his own company. Or you will see him going over to the client company and become a buyer.
  There is a famous case of a guy who was a creative director doing advertising for a big client, I think it was for Canon in Holland. He became the person responsible for strategy inside the company and stopped doing creative stuff and then he became the buyer. He stepped over entirely to Canon, and he became the client.'

'Most of the designers will not do that kind of stuff, they simply can't do it because they're not good enough. The other thing you can do is - like I did - step back in the other direction again once you realise the step you have taken.'

'I used to be interested in management but then I realised it was not my world. It doesn't interest me in terms of my personal development. I went back to making things.'

regional towards the formation of trans-regional identity it seems important to talk, write or visualise in an accessible understandable language. The simply structured, generally understandable mega-productions of the film industry succeed globally. Language and imagery are internationalised.

'That's why you left Hard Werken [design studio/ed.] at the point where they became more commercial and merged with the packaging company?'

'How long did that take?'

'In 1985 there was a financial crisis wasn't there?'

'They were going down too, or was that later?'

'I think there are certain things you can only learn through making mistakes or through stupidity and experience.'

'Yes, through experience! You can't learn that in school, can you?'

'No, it had actually already happened before that. I stepped down and I reorganised myself, a year before they merged.'

'If you are to talking about the merger you have to go back to 1988, that was 8 years ago.'

'In 1986 there was a financial crisis. We started to look for partners around '88, and I think it was in 1989 that Total Design tried to buy us.'

'I think that all happened at the same time. They were going down and at the same time they were opening up companies in Paris and Brussels. They simply needed some fresh air in the company. We talked with a lot of different companies. We got a new financial director in 1991. As soon as this man entered I decided to step down. I removed myself from the management side. After that, of course, the work for the JvE (Jan van Eyck Akademie) started. I had already seen the kind of work I could do and I had already learned a lot of that stuff, but I could also see that it was definitely not for me. I mean, I paid for college myself, I had jobs to get experience, and I ended up being a clerk again, a high level clerk, but I was still a clerk. It was like having an office job, just talking with people, dealing, selling, and not working for yourself, not making things literally with your own hands. It seemed as though it was just a romantic notion to want to make things with your hands, because there was no money in it, you would earn much more doing other things.'

'Or by looking at the work of others, or working in the field.'

'I think the biggest mistake at the JvE is... that they say that to conceptualise is a textual thing and that if you conceptualise on a textual basis — which most people in advertising do — it makes you more flexible towards what you are working on. But if you are only working with your own technique and you're limited to one mode of expression then it will limit you in the way you deal with clients. It might provide you with very strong criteria for selecting clients, but in my own experience that leads to a life of poverty.
 Look at it from the functionalist point of view. People in advertising fall into two groups, visual designers and copy designers, and this is because each aspect has its own particular set of problems. One person will be better at understanding one thing, while another will be better at understanding the other. If they make a good team they will compensate for each other's weaknesses.'

I do not see a problem in the connection between commerce and culture, I find the problem lies in the lack of consciousness in dealing with communication. It is more appealing to dive into virtual and unreal fantasy worlds than to face reality in a constructive way. Information does not move people

**anymore.** The flood of information via world-wide nets and the consequent illusion of global necessity creates an infinite indifferent abstract in which the illusionist messages of the advertising world find a new breeding ground. The term 'infotainment' unmasks itself as a serious concern. If graphic

'Yeah, but that's how big advertising companies developed, or that's how they started because two people like Meire & Meire in Germany who were very successful in the Eighties had a marketing side and a creative side.'

'They had a creative side, but the creative part was divided into text and image. Basically they would say that if you were visually oriented you would have to find ways of becoming more flexible towards what you do. And the way to do that is not to contextualise, but to 'textualise'. That word doesn't really exist but I guess it is appropriate. We come back to hard commercial practice. The rhetoric of the text seems to be in a much stronger negotiating position than the rhetoric of the image. An example of this is the neon sequence I did for the PTT. It was a completely visual concept, but still I had to go back and textualise the thing.'

'How did you do that?'

'By analysing it.'

'How?'

'What do you mean how? By looking at what I did and trying to read what the story was.'

'What was the story?'

'There are two stories. There's a true story and there's a true lie. I did this print for them for the commemoration of the thing, the true story comes out, it's called the 'Rise and Fall of the house style PTT'. In the neon display, there are three PTT logos. But you can't see them all properly because the logo comes up like the sun and disappears into the night. The logo that comes up like the sun is very clear; it says PTT, and it's very hard-edged, and so clear that you can still read it when it's going off. Whereas the last image - it's a sequence of five images - is their house style for KPN and PTT Post, which is completely engulfed in these little things that you used to have, designed all around it like circles; and it's completely lost in there. It's much smaller, it gets lost in the night. It's even smaller than the moon which is there too. That's why it's called 'Rise and Fall of the house style PTT'. It's an epic neon.'

'In the lecture that you and Anthon gave at the JvE, Anthon mentioned the fact that incredible luck has been part of his career – particularly in his client structure. What do you do, do you plan your client structure or do things just happen? I was thinking of your job for the Kunstmuseum Wolfsburg which opened three years ago, where you supervised their publicity and PR activities from the start. That was a unique opportunity, very few people get the chance to have such a wonderful job.'

'There is chance but not in the sense of luck. I mean in this case the client initially came to me for advice.'

81

**design wants to clarify the complexity of political happenings and decision making, and if it wants to lessen the rational and cunning behaviour of capitalism it has to make a contribution to sensitisation and emotionalisation. This is only possible if the profession tries to demystify itself**

continued on page 84

'Before the competition?'

'Yes, and I advised him to hold the competition. At first, I tried to get him to take on my company, but he wouldn't go for that, and then I advised him to hold a competition and I entered the competition as well. I helped set up the competition and I also mentioned Studio Anthon Beeke and Grapus in Paris and two other people took part as well. Ott & Stein were probably told about it by somebody in Hannover. Gijs (van Tuyl, director of Kunstmuseum Wolfsburg) himself wanted to have Peter Schmidt because he likes Hugo Boss and Peter Schmidt designs for Hugo Boss. I entered my work and I won because mine was the best. Usually, when you set up a competition, and take part in it yourself, you don't win. In this case, I won because the other designs didn't have the same potential to survive outside the museum. That was something I had worked on because I had absorbed the problem very well and I knew I had to develop something that could lead a life of its own outside the museum. The others simply didn't do that, they referred to the location or to this particular museum, whereas I decided to work on the notion of curating or the notion of a museum in general.'

'I often hear that you are unhappy about the grant situation. Is all design in Holland made possible through big financial input from the government?'

'No, no, no. Let's be clear about this, I think that the subsidisers have the wrong strategy. The money usually goes to the people who are young, who have been out of art school for two years, and this won't really help the designer because of the way they give the subsidies and how they are assessed. They help the wrong way round; they give somebody an impetus to look at himself and what he is working for. Sometimes that creates a very big gap between the designer and the market he is working for. It has to do with the fact that this grant system is not really designed for graphic designers, it's developed for architects, artists, and people who work in industrial design, and in what they call 'autonomous design' – pottery, glasswork. With these it's completely different because in one year you can develop a product that can be put on the market. Most graphic designers can't do that. They hardly use the grant to get a better idea of what they are actually working towards. As Marie Helene Cornips said recently to somebody, these grants should be used for designers of about my age, let's say accomplished designers, to take a sabbatical for a year or two.'

'Like a free experimental year.'

'Yeah, something like that. But the fact that they could apply for it is not really published. They have an income limit, which is something like fifty or sixty thousand before tax. This makes it impossible for a lot of people to apply because they earn too much.'

'Your main interest is in fine arts, that's what you studied. Do you do artwork for yourself in your free time?'

'I don't have any free time.'

'So you could apply for a grant.'

'I make too much money to apply for a grant. I would have to do very badly for one year and then I could apply for a grant. For me it's different. I am planning to do something, but I'm not going to use their money to buy freedom for myself. If you have a company like mine the turnover is like 35,000 – 40,000 a month. The grant would only provide me with one and a half month's freedom if I stopped working. So, what's the point? It's not like when you are on a salary and you quit for one year. When you are self employed and you have a company this salary question is not really applicable. But what I am going to do is develop my own project and ask for a project grant. Which is a way of planning your own work and getting society to pay for it. Like Anthon did with his atelier project which he presented at the Stedelijk a couple of years ago; he did a kind of forensic surgeon's studio.

'What will you do?'

'OK.'

'You too have a love-hate relationship with your profession?'

'I mentioned these grants because Wolfsburg is also an example where a huge amount of money is available which makes this graphic design possible. Would that fall away if the money were not there?'

'No, I mean what they put into advertising makes it what it is.'

'You plan the advertising and publicity strategy for one year with them?'

'Yeah, that's, by the way, what I have suffered from since I've been here. I mean whatever you put on the table at the JvE, they always say 'nice', and then this whole critique starts again. They can never be very enthusiastic about the product. In my eye, that's a big problem in graphic design too, that the theory is there but no one concentrates on the results. The process is private and I want to keep it to myself.'

'What was your idea when you started there?'

'I'm not prepared to talk about that.'

'But it has nothing to do with design, absolutely nothing.'

'Yeah!'

'Well, Wolfsburg is less than half of my work.'

'Well, it's getting less and less; two years ago they spent 2 million DM on advertising, but now the budget is four or five hundred thousand or three hundred thousand. What I am doing for them is the traditional stuff, catalogues and posters, and I do little ads for them. These ads are designed twice a year, they are housestyle ads which you don't have to design.'

'No, that's what they do, they have an advertising and publicity manager, Dr. Maria Schneider, and she is doing ads, posters and invitations as part of her work. She is working most of the time with the press, with journalists, to prepare press conferences and on the magazines. She's doing a very good job. This museum gets incredible coverage. If you look at Carl Andre who is absolutely no novelty, they've had a lot of press.
In the Dutch situation, they would only have been nagging about this place. But the Germans are a little bit like Americans, so if something is new and interesting, they are interested in it, they don't moralize straight away. That's one of the diseases of the Dutch situation, everybody moralizes about things all the time.'

'Yeah, being in school means that you have to try to be a little bit transparent. I don't see any harm in that, but it's more the other thing. I mean I really don't know what the JvE is about, I don't know what they want to do, I was there for a couple for years, and I really don't know what Jan's (Jan van Toorn) idea is about.'

y

'My idea was that I should make. I had a very simple objective, and Jan and I shared this objective. So I thought we could really work together on that. But his approach wasn't mine and my experiences were not valued enough to function as new, let's say, paradigms, which could be developed further in this institution. Jan's agenda was always more important than the agenda I could develop for myself. The other thing was that I got completely disoriented towards design through this process and I still am. I think if you want to do this, what they do at the JvE, you need people from advertising there. I think it's interesting if you have people like Max Kisman, but you need people who are really working in the commercial field. If you make theoretical and even visual work it stays on a theoretical level because it can't

and, adopting a healthy relationship between rationality and
complaining about a lack of acceptance do not lead forward.
using its own instrumentality, to shift the viewpoint and to c
itself.

function outside. That's a kind of limitation and I think that in that way you will train teachers and not designers. I think Jan's hidden agenda is that he wants to train teachers and he knows that it will take another generation before this teaching can be brought to reality.

A few days ago, I saw a programme on television and there was the director of the Whitney Museum. This man is completely nuts, completely over the top, he said things about the Internet, about interactive communication. There's a huge setting up of a new exclusive system. This man says that if you're sitting on a couch and watching a movie it is passive, but if you are sitting in front of a computer and fucking Internet or wanking Internet this is active. This man is the director of the Whitney so he must have had very good training, he must be a master in philosophy and history, and he talks the most incredible nonsense. He's one of these Internet fever cases. I think it's a hype that will pass after a short time. If you look at the development of high tech funds, you know, high tech stock funds, you can see that the hype is over. I'm worried about what this man says, they are talking about the need for a new type of person. As if the salvation of the world depends on it.

I remember this Dutch writer Gerard Reve who once talked about the right to silence. He was getting sick of the fact that in every cafe there were people playing music, playing radios and that you could never walk outside without hearing a radio. Lots of people now would say this is an archaic idea because people don't know anymore what it's like to have silence, just silence.

But this ridiculous person also demands the coming of the age of a human type who is locked into this silly thing which is a tool, not a way of life. They try to make us believe that it's a way of life. That is sad, very sad.'

'Yeah, it's very sad. And if you look at most of these examples...'

'The biggest problem is that when people are not working, not moving their hands, they're not processing. I remember when I worked in the harbour as a student, most of the time you had nothing to do but you were not allowed to read a book because if you read, you were sitting down and they could see that you were not doing anything. So what you had to do was to walk around, pretend to work. Now, if you are looking at a screen and processing mentally what you see there, you have to answer to that. It's ridiculous.

The other thing I remember was that designers began to protest heavily against testing, the testing of products, the testing of design, like the stamps - their communicative level. They started five years ago and there was a big uprising among designers because it was like the second coming of Adolf Hitler. Marketing seemed to have touched the same mental chord in designers. If you listen to this man and you listen to what he anticipates the net will do, it all has to do with success and functionality. It all has to do with a very quick response by people to things because this response will decide whether or not they will continue to view your product. You will be complimented on that. This means that designers become more and more functional than ever, there is more and more of a limit on what you can call individual expression or whatever. These same people who are against marketing and testing, these people are advocates of the Internet and interface. They simply don't know the reality of what they are doing.

Gui Bonsiepe knows, but he's not a romantic, he's a very functional man. He has high ideals, but they all lie within what the tool can do, they do not lie within what he can do on a level of expression with the tool. Maybe he can do it, I don't know.'

on, presents itself to a broad public. Self-indulgence and
an opportunity here for approaching the advertising domain
the notion of reality within a system by using the medium

'There's a difference between talking and doing, if you see Gui talking and developing theories, they sound very interesting and very complex, but at the end of the day, what is on the table?'

'Edition, exactly! This book is called View to the Future; can you give your personal view to the future for young people?'

'What will be your field of action in the year 2000?'

'I can understand it because it does take an entire generation of technicians and conceptualists who will work together and will do the real interface design in ten years' time. That's not my problem. My biggest problem is that the advocates of the internet are the same people who are against any type of consumer influence in what they do, yet they enter a medium that will make consumers influence the law. There's no way of getting away from that. You will have your Internet homepage just for yourself, in your own room. Here I will have my connection to the Internet and you will be sitting there, we both look into each other's homepage, and nobody else will look at it because they don't give a shit. It will be the same as art school, you will say: 'People don't understand my work, but at least you do, let's get another beer'. You understand what I mean? You get back to the notion of the art world, you say I only need one person who understands.

But with design it's different, one person understanding doesn't pay. The main thing is that designers get paid through the fractionalisation of their service. If you are a creative director on Huggie's, then your fee is being paid through three cents of every package. If you buy a Jeff Koons, you have to pay him the full amount of money, the $2,000,000. Then you are the only one to have this Jeff Koons. This is basically the biggest difference between art and design.'

'It depends on whether you want to be a designer or not. That means that this view is only interesting if you can be a generalist, that's my strong point. You can only become a generalist with a very wide understanding of things – this will also buy you freedom in a way. You have to focus very strongly on what you think it is a designer does, you have to develop that. It could also be that you are an interface designer working only with a writer, with a scenario writer, you have to orientate yourself. If I were to orientate myself as an interface designer, knowing my character, I would become more interested in cinematic graphics, if I were a master in working with sequences, I would become a filmmaker.'

'It's not so far off, it's only three years. I'm not sure. I think for me, on a personal level, it's a very interesting question because I think I will continue to develop myself and I'm not sure in what field I will be working. But I earn my money with design and you have to survive as well. I simply don't know where it will take me. I'm doing more and more photography. But being a designer you always think in terms of projects, you will focus on a given moment to create a given project. I have some things in mind that I want to do with visual culture, it all has to do with visual culture. I'm not going to sell groceries or something like that.

On one hand I give strategic consultancy to clients, that's something uncommon and in my view that's how graphic designers should function in the future, if they can develop that way. On the other hand, I'm working in a totally traditional niche of the market. I think this traditional niche of the market can allow me to live and survive for the coming thirty years. I think, and you have seen this in the past, that whenever there is a moment when the book is being challenged as a product, there is a renewed emphasis on the quality of the book. In the field of literature, books will not disappear very quickly. Reference books, books on sailing, gardening... can actually be better on a CD-ROM. If you are talking about difficult representational aspects like art catalogues, the experience of a book is important because of the level of contemplation the subject demands, etc. There is an aspect of added value that you can create by certain technical specifications that you can give to the book. I think these aspects will remain for some decades. To make a good book is more and more expensive. Printers are charging less, but the costs of things like paper has tripled over the past five years. When something gets expensive there is always a diminution in the number of people who can afford it, but on the other hand, there always remains a kind of exclusivity which will create a limited market. One lesson to be learned from the 80's and the 90's, is that commercially speaking, specialisations are really important.'

'But you just said that you can only survive if you're a generalist, so that's a contradiction.'

'No, I'm talking about the book and different products.'

'Then you have to be both.'

'If you're a good book designer, then you're already a generalist, because you are able to work with complicated contents and editorials. You are already an editor, you edit design. If you're not good at editing design, you cannot become a good book designer. So, there is already that aspect of generalism there. Now it's a different situation, you have a strategy for yourself and you can also look at the market you can work for. Being a good book designer is something that you can also use when you develop other things with your own work. Your skill will not be completely lost.'

'How important is a certain kind of education? Does language get affected by global language, as via the internet every national border vanishes? There is a language developed out of a computer-engineer-vocabulary. Do you think this leads to dumbness?'

'I think that more people are much more educated than they were fifty years ago. You always hear complaints that the level of this education is not what it used to be. But I cannot really judge that because I do not have such a good education.'

'You gave a good education to yourself, didn't you?'

'Yeah, but it would be very good if I had a classic, humanistic education. I think that's very important. Fewer and fewer people get that education. Even people who have a good basic education still get it from their parents, or from the interests their parents implant in them to develop that. I think that the proportion of people who really get a classic education is maybe five percent.'

'What are your inner conflicts and when are you personally fulfilled?'

'That is the last question. Do I get a year to answer this? I very rarely experience fufilment. Most of the time you're a good designer if you have a bigger appetite than you can afford. You will find, unlike in fine arts and music, your boundaries come from the clients you work for and that's why there are many unhappy designers. You can quote this bicentennial lecture from Lorraine Wild. I never want to let this happen to me, but I am very aware of what happened to Paul Rand and others of his generation. They got all the fame, the acknowledgement and the money they wanted, but they all turned out to be these incredibly bitter old men who felt completely lost. There are two reasons for this, one is what she calls the brilliant child who doesn't get understood by its parents and who develops a constant eagerness to please other people. That seems to be central to designers. The other is, of course with design, unlike art and architecture, what you do, however brilliant, always gets swamped by other stuff, by time, it disappears. It's nowhere. You have to be very strong to be able to carry that.'

'THANKYOU FOR THIS TALK!'

Jop van Bennekom
Too close for comfort

Lex Reitsma

An article about the work of dutch designer

# Lex Reitsma

**by Jop van Bennekom**

presenting ;-) ---------------------------------------------- (1:1)
a book in a book /

# Too close for -
# comfort

start >>

title:              Aarsman's Amsterdam
photography:        Hans Aarsman 1992
text:               Hans Aarsman © 1989 - 1992
bookdesign:         Lex Reitsma, Haarlem
typesetting:        W. Groot bv, Amsterdam
lithography:        Evertsen Repro Service bv, Hoofddorp
printed by:         Lecturis bv, Eindhoven
binding:            Epping bv, Woerden

published by:       Bookshop De Verbeelding

first edition: april 1993

------------------------------------------------------------

CIP-Gegevens Koninklijke Bibliotheek Den Haag

Aarsman, Hans
Aarsman's Amsterdam: foto's en notities/ Hans Aarsman
Amsterdam: boekhandel De Verbeelding - foto's
ISBN 90-74159-04-4 (hardcover)
ISBN 90-74159-05-2 (paperback)
NUGI 922
Trefwoord: Amsterdam; fotoboeken.

1

< Censored parts incl. >

Why do things look the way they do? Few publications in the field of graphic design would be able to answer this question. Maybe it is not their intention to formulate an answer to this question, but it irritates me that design is often described from a single, mostly visual, point of view; it conditions us in part after all. That irritation is reason enough for me to make the question the subject of this article, to regard the finished product as central, using the same limitations as so-called coffeetable books. Vaguely conscious of the Eastern wisdom that 'something' can hold 'everything', I attempt to describe the book in its totality; an 'interview' with a book.

## 01. to analyse

The book I am analysing for this article is in oblong format, meaning a format horizontal in character. A book in oblong format is always already a code; it immediately signals that we are dealing here with a photobook, a book about landscape or, of course, about landscape photography. The overall view you have of the double page of an oblong book is strongly dependent on its format and proportions. On initial measurement it appeared to have the standard A4 format.

A4 (1:15)                    A4 horizontal (1:15)

Standard A4 is often seen as an all too common format, the editor's format; manuscript is almost always handed in in A4. It is the format with which design starts and in this case it is left like that, save that the vertical has been made horizontal. As well as banal, A4 is often considered 'ugly' by many designers; I never understood why. A4 works, if only because we always deal with it in our working environment yet no longer find it in the bookshop, as if everything always has to be made special. The choice of this format has to be conscious, no designer chooses 210 x 297 mm by accident. It is also

2

very disadvantageous to print; because of the proportions less pages fit on a printing page; you are left with more surplus paper and, of course, less money.

I have always had a problem with oblong books and all the more with those of considerable size like this one; it is hard to fit on the book shelf. If you want to place it in its original horizontal position in a row of books it protrudes considerably; one can live with that but, it does make the book very loudly present. That is why I often shelve an oblong book vertically, but then you do not see the spine, only the cut pages. The fate of a book without a spine and so without identity is that it is quickly forgotten. How many oblong books live a twilight existence next to many very present counter-parts? It becomes a choice between a very present and an almost anonymous book.

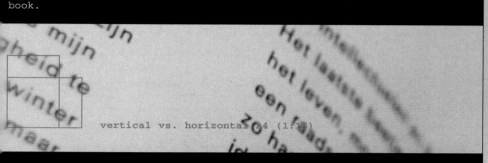

vertical vs. horizontal 0.4 (1:1.3)

This book is of considerable size; 136 pages inside and a rather thick hard cover on paper of 250 g approx. There is a dust jacket around the cover itself for protection. All this makes it a book of 11 mm approx. Inside there are 11 quires, sewn and glued into the cover (paperback). The book is half text and half photographs. Text and photos are alternated per quire. The five photo quires are printed on 170 g approx. coated paper, the six text quires on a thinner 120 g approx. uncoated paper. Using coated paper for photographs and uncoated paper for text is done often, particularly in exhibition catalogues. Coated paper makes the photos sharper and brighter; on uncoated paper the colours are somewhat subdued. Particularly with this book it is essential for the print of the photograph to be perfect. Text on uncoated paper makes a text page more tangible and tactile. Often it is the case that the paper is off-white in colour giving just a little less contrast between the white of the paper and the black of the type. This is much more comfortable to read. Using the combination of coated paper for photographs and uncoated for text does however constitute a value judgement, a hierarchy you get for nothing. Particularly in this case where the photos are printed on thicker paper.

3

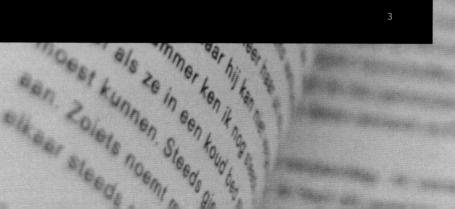

## 02. to cover

The dust jacket is made of the same paper as the photo quires and consists of two flaps folded around the hard cover, each flap being exactly half A4 in format. Then there are the front and back covers and the spine of again 11 mm.

dust jacket (1:15)

The front of the dust jacket, which in fact serves as the cover, shows a landscape photograph, bled-off on four sides and printed in full colour, the title Aarsman's Amsterdam and the name of the publisher, De Verbeelding. The title of the book is set in heavy, black, sanserif capitals in a proportionally rather large body of type. The two words of the title are detached and placed one beneath the other whereby 'Amsterdam' is set in a larger type face than 'Aarsman's' and is centred on the page. The word 'Aarsman's' is not centred but shifted a few centimetres in relation to the word 'Amsterdam'. It would have been very logical for it to have been centred as well, because the name of the publisher 'De Verbeelding', cut into the photograph, is set in a smaller typeface but in the same sanserif capitals and vertically centred to the right. Why, you then ask yourself, is 'Aarsman's' not centred? Not that design always has to be based entirely on logic, but these are the sort of irritations which are hardly bearable when you think about it too much. Like one yellow brick in a red brick wall.

The photo on the jacket, in full colour, is of an ordinary street with office blocks, probably taken from one of the office blocks on the other side. Because the word 'Amsterdam' is in big letters on the jacket you instantly and logically presume that we are dealing here with a photo of Amsterdam, which is indeed the case; you are looking at the Wibautstraat. It is not a photo of Amsterdam like those we know so well from pictures of cosy canals and bright flower stalls. No, this is almost the Amsterdam you do not want to know about, partly because it is not specific; the Wibautstraat could be anywhere; in Delfzijl or Heerlen. It is actually a very grim photograph of a

4

noman's land where only cars race past and people are locked up in offices along a semi-motorway in the centre of town. In the photograph some people are walking about, cars stop at traffic lights, another car is just going round the corner; a representation of something we have in fact already known for so long.

The cover photograph invites you to start quickly leafing through the book. It acts almost as a starting point; a point at which nothing is happening yet, the real work starts inside. In fact the whole book contains the sort of photos in which nothing special can be seen. I get the impression it was a very conscious decision for the cover to give only a very limited amount of information; textually it is limited to title and publisher; no sales talk and no notion of the cover as a 'hilarious highlight', an eruption of the content inside. You can almost see that the designer had difficulty inserting the title into the cover photograph; suddenly the photo was no longer the photo because text had been added. Maybe in this case it would have been better not to have text at all, just the photo.

But a photograph does not have a loud voice and does not let itself be contextualised so easily. It can't say, for instance, 'Hans Aarsman took me, this is about Amsterdam and so-and-so is the publisher of this book.' Which is why text is needed.

The dust jacket was originally intended to protect the cover under-neath it. With old books a whole world is often hidden behind the jacket, often more abstract and tactile (blind stamp, linen-bound, etc.) as if the jacket is a facade and the book can be itself again when it has been removed. In this case the original cover has been left blank and the question arises as to why it had to be protected at all. There is a discrepancy between the actual reason for having a dust jacket and the way in which I see it being used more and more often these days. I think the fact that there are more and more blank covers hidden behind dust jackets is due merely to economic consider-ations; printing the cover is costly and when the dust jacket can be printed together with the inside pages, as in this instance, why spend extra money to have the thicker paper printed?

I often remove dust jackets; they get crumpled with intensive use or slide off the book if they are made of coated paper. But most of the time I cannot throw a jacket away; a little too much care has gone into it for that and, after all, whichever way you look at it, it is part of the book. The big problem with removing dust jackets is that you do not really have a place to keep them. Not everything has to have its place, but one way or another the lost or, rather, discarded dust jackets do not find a home; they belong on the bookshelf but, spineless as they are, rather like the memory of a content they can only circumscribe, they cannot settle there either. It is always a particular sort of jacket that cannot find its place. It is awful when a book is 'portrayed' too simplistically; for one reason or another the depiction always falls short of encompassing the whole story whilst the designer tries desperately to simplify the whole caboodle, to be contained in one glance at a jacket. Maybe it is better to deny the dust jacket its status and regard it as the beginning of the content rather than a resume or pithy detail in which much nuance is lost.

I always find, as a designer, the interior of a book much more interesting than the cover; the decisions one takes (if, of course, you have that freedom) happen more on an editing level. And it is exactly at that level that the designer can really put his thinking to use. Everybody has his place in the production process: writer, publisher, editor, designer and photographer. And they all want as well to protect that position because it simplifies the process; why would a designer get involved in the subeditor's business?

These hierarchies often give rise to situations in which the designer is called in to do the job at the very last minute so that he has to throw the idea quickly into shape without really being involved. It is not surprising then that most design floats some-

6

94

where near the surface and that a marked distance is kept: design as the obligatory finishing touch, the cherry on the cake.

I recently discovered that, with a bit of folding, a dust jacket can be turned inside out. As most dust jackets are left blank inside, this gives a nice row of blank books. Just imagine that traditionally dust jackets would not exist and all books appeared in white, blank and abstract; you would only recognise a book by its proportions.

There are people with a strong nostalgia for a lost time in which the word 'bibliophile' still meant something, who wrap their (often hardback) books in brown wrapping paper and then write the title on the spine with a quill or some other nostalgic writing tool. I can't blame them; it is a pity that dust jackets are designed merely for their function in the shop, as sales tool, and at home you have to find out for yourself whether you feel queasy when you see an all too explicit jacket for the fiftieth time.

## 03. to represent

Before concentrating on the interior of the book I first have to say something about the content of the book by which one can evaluate the design. On the back cover of the dust jacket is a short description of the content:

'For a year he had been roaming through the Netherlands in a camper-van (resulting in the photobook Hollandse Taferelen (Dutch Tableaux) published in 1989). Returning to Amsterdam, his native city, he recognised everything but saw it with new eyes. The old and familiar was presented to him anew. What harm can come to me, he thought over-confidently.'

He in this case is Hans Aarsman, photographer and writer. And the book contains his photographs and short notes. The notes seem to come out of a diary, sometimes they are observations of daily life but more often personal confidences from his private life. In the notes a story unravels about recurring relationship perils and a struggle with his work as a photographer, of which the book is the final result. Two quotations from the notes have stuck with me and represent well the intention with which he takes pictures:

'The intake is an illusion. A photograph takes on a subject auto-matically, whether you put it in beforehand or not. Because in time all photos, including the meaningless ones, will have something special. ... But see it as an aim or a way of working. To be faster than my intentions, to stay ahead of thought. Not to let myself be lured into an opinion. And, well, in a world so full of them nobody will miss one or two little opinions. And this is how I continue my search for photographs which are not for anyone's convenience.'

'The here and now will never get the regard it deserves, the great attention is directed towards what is elsewhere in space and time.'

This is in fact untilled ground; the field of daily life, the here and now, the things nobody finds important enough to capture. Hans Aarsman makes an attempt with this book. These are photos in which, at first glance, nothing is happening. The very fact that one is always looking for a rarification, a removal from daily life, makes these photos even more rare. You keep looking and searching for something special and in the meantime you take such a good look at these photographs like you have never done with your own surroundings. Your gaze is intensified and you become conscious of the fact that you never really look around. Aarsman's work expresses the longing to connect life and work to such an extent that there is no longer any distinction or hierarchy; detours are no longer taken so that everything, simply and directly, flows from itself. The moment you become one with your surroundings.

## 04. to design

The interior consists, as I mentioned earlier, of six quires of uncoated white paper of 120 g approx. for text (notes) and five quires of double-sided coated paper of 170 g approx. for the photographs. The text quires have eight and the photo quires sixteen pages. The photos are treated in the same way throughout the book; bled-off on all sides whereby the left page, being the back of the preceding photograph, has been left blank apart from an almost invisible indication of the location of the photo next to it. This is placed on the right 14 mm from the bottom, printed in a relatively small type.

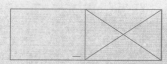

spread (1:15)

When we start to think from the point of the photo and text material again, with which after all a book begins, a number of rather logical and easily discernable decisions have been taken by the designer. The photos for instance are not suitable for framing, they do not warrant an explicit treatment or positioning and, because they are

8

bled-off, and so fill the entire page, become an enclosed reality, as if the photograph is a randomly chosen part of a greater whole which you can no longer see but which is present in thought. In other words, it is as if the photo continues and therefore it is good also that it is on the right-hand page with the left-hand page left blank each time. This leaves the eye free to roam over the photograph and does not force upon us extra meaning in the form of metaphor which always arises when two images are placed next to one another.

The print quality of the photographs is excellent. I think a lot of work has gone into the translation to print of the intensity and the light of the photograph. The colours of the photos almost question the way you look; are these really the colours and the light of my daily surroundings or have they been manipulated? In print from the Fifties you often see that photos are very colourful; did people then think that reality too was as 'colourful' or was this more related to the technical limitations of printing at that time?

In this book image and text are explicitly separated and this is not without reason; text and image cannot really cope with one another. In everyday reality one hardly notices how they naturally blend into one another and obtain, or not, mutual meaning. The moment they become artefacts in the sense of photographs or text they lose this logic. The abstraction of the typography and the figurativity of the photo each stem from a different world and in a book they are brought together. Even now with the whole 'digital revolution' whereby the technical possibilities of integrating image and text are greater than ever, this opposition remains. We want to overcome the separation of text but we can't. I often ask myself what would happen if writing were to be invented now, in 1997.

One could imagine that text and image in this design could be put in a relation other than rigid separation. But maybe it is very right that the photographs stand completely alone and do not enter into a visual relation with either other photographs or text. In the way a book communicates one should not overlook how looking at image and reading text each follow different paths from those signalled by the analogue structures and relative postionings of the design. This is often overlooked in discussions about design; as if people perceive in the same way that a designer designs. But the question is how explicit are you; is a book not after all a context in which information functions? Making the tools, one has as a designer, work in relation to each other and showing their coherence or incoherence can broaden the scope of meaning, which gives people the chance to relate to the work on another level than where everything is presented separately, as it is here.

9

The choice in this design not to place, for instance, all texts at the front and all photos at the back is also a decision based on creating variety within the whole. Separating texts and photos would also deny their inter-relation, whereas this is very clearly present and adds value to both text and photos. The choice of basing the division of the book on the alternate use of a text quire of 8 pages and a photo quire of 16 pages is therefore a very logical one. The fact that a limited amount of photos and text were available for this publication already partly dictates this choice. As a quire has to be folded and cut in four or eight it then consists not of seven or seventeen but of eight and sixteen pages. Quires of eight or sixteen are very common and so it is in this design.

One quire with sixteen continuous pages of text would be too much for the available amount of text in this design. You would either have to double the size of the photo quire, and so lose the variation between text and image (nor does it fit with the available amount of photographs), or you would have to double the size of the text quire only. But a doubling of the amount of space for the text would mean the text would 'run out' very soon while the photos would still continue, in which case you would have to opt for a rather large type for the text and enormous white margins around it. So, we have eight consecutive text pages which also works better on the level of orientation within the book; it is harder to get lost in eight pages of text than in sixteen. Orientation is important in this book because the treatment of the text is rather uniform and the notes read and function differently than, for instance, the analogue text continuity in a novel. Let us therefore presume for the sake of convenience that from the point of view of bookmaking technique the decisions on the final design are logical or in any case that they ensue logically from the content. No codes or conventions are stretched here.

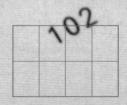

plano 16 page quire (1:30)

In the first text quire the first four pages are reserved for the opening page, a word of acknowledgement, the title page and a dedication (in that order), after which come the eight pages of text. The

10

last, sixth, text quire concludes with four pages with the colophon on one and the rest left blank. There is therefore created, by division, a completely symmetrical book. As well as text and photos affirming themselves, the book does so too in its overall symmetrical form.

## 05. to type

I find typography one of the most difficult areas in the practice of the graphic designer. Not so much construction of the typographic make-up, on the contrary, in fact, because of all the handy computer programmes, one is seduced into very quickly making something that 'looks good'. Making a typographic proposal based on content is a form of abstract thinking not everyone is inclined to. You relate to a content, a text, on an abstract level; in the choice of typeface, pagination, the placing of headings and footnotes etcetera. One has to sharpen all those references that will give the text an appearance of its own as well as the intended layers of meaning. But it is exact- ly the quoting and referring needed to arrive at a typographic appearance that I have a problem with in modern typography. It is almost as if letters cannot be themselves anymore because they are always deliberately chosen, quoted from the great jukebox of typo- graphic tradition. Maybe this is why I see typography more and more as styling, put figuratively in quotation-marks. Were there better times? Typographic nostalgia itself is the biggest quotation imaginable, but there were times when the face of a letter related to the technique used. We are now left with completely different reproduction techniques and burdened with quotations and references from, for example, the sixteenth century; text as image.

In the design of this article, for instance, Courier has been used. A typing letter originally used on the already outdated type writers and now digitalised.

**Courier 18 pt.**

Courier 18 pt. >> **The position of typographic tradition and text itself is now being rapidly eroded. Image is starting to dominate increasingly because image is faster, faster as a communicator; in one glance you read an image and assign meaning to it. Text is much slower in this. And at times of information overload you want to have quick access to information, on the one hand, to be able to select it and on the other to take it in.**

Returning to the typography of this book, the decisions, as in the case of the design, are easy to discern. Let us first establish that the composition of a typographic make-up for an oblong-sized book is a different matter than for a book with a standard format, especially when an oblong book has a relatively large format like horizontal A4 (297 x 210 mm). You are almost forced to use several columns in the design because otherwise the lines become too long and one gets lost reading them; at the end of a line it becomes hard to find where the next one starts.

Two or more columns seems obvious; for this design two columns has been chosen, again perhaps a logical option. Three columns are awkward in a carefully designed book; you have to read every page three times, as it were. In a magazine the use of multiple columns has an entirely different function than in a book. In this design the use of two columns works in favour of those texts which consist of short notes. They read in a more detached way and stand more in cross-relation to one another than if they were simply placed one beneath the other. The notes follow, a white line separating one from the next, one directly behind the other. Because all sections are of a different length and size, more flexibility is needed than if all columns had the same number of lines. Steps have been taken to avoid the last line of a second column ending up on the second page or, worse, the last word not fitting. Those widows can be very confusing for the reader and can break the aesthetics of typographic design. This has been avoided in this design by making the column length flexible with a maximum of 27 text lines. Even more flexibility has been built in to fit the text into the typographic design; the text has for instance been set in non-aligned margins so that words can be shifted to the next line when this is more suitable.

Within typography white plays an important role; what is not there plays aesthetically as important a role as what is there, i.e. the text. It is precisely the creation of such typographic fields of tension, the careful dosing of relationships and the playing out of oppositions against one another, which determines the architecture of typography. Within the design of this book these fields of tension are a bit lost in the large masses of white around the columns. The horizontal character of the typography has been emphasized by choosing large white spaces above and underneath the text. But then no real choice has been made for an explicit horizontal appearance, for this the white spaces to the right and left of the text columns

12

are just a little too large to set the horizon and to enter into relationship with the next (or former) page. You always have to consider a typographic design as a spread, a double page. The two columns start to float a little in the middle of the page as if they do not want to relate to the paper nor to the format and thus to the book in its entirety. This is just as much emphasized by the page number dangling loose underneath the first column as by the column of white between the first and second text columns. The page number stands in direct relation to the text, which is unusual, generally it relates to the page.

The tail gutter is a little larger than the heads, which is common because otherwise it seems as if the text is dropping off the page and disturbing the balance. Text placed just a little above the centre of the page seems to anchor it in the white and thus in the page. Text, in the typographic idiom, always enters into battle with the white, typography always seems to be an attempt to attach text to a field; anchoring something as abstract as a series of signs with the physical and material character of a limited piece of paper in a book.

The choice of setting the texts rather passively in a field is most likely a choice against explicit articulation rather than a choice for a certain kind of articulation. The text is almost not articulated at all; totally uniform, it ripples along and probably no longer bears any relation to the diary scribbles one imagines these notes must have been originally.

The typeface used throughout the book is Akzidenz Grotesk; one of the oldest sanserif typefaces, issued in 1898 by the German type-foundry Berthold. Most sanserif typefaces were originally based on this, a still very useful fore-runner. Akzidenz Grotesk may be a dry, businesslike face, but it has just that little bit extra character and is less mechanical than the often-used derivatives Helvetica and Univers. In this design the typeface has been used in a rather sub-dued manner, not too big and not too small; the chosen body is exactly in proportion with the format of the book and the amount of text on a page. The lettertype has also been rather widely spaced and the line space is proportionally rather large. All these may seem rather neutral measures to make typography neutral but in the meantime the whole book does acquire a meaning beyond its scope. The book moves in the typographic idiom always used in museum catalogues. An idiom based on a retiring and servile role for the designer, even if it is coming to show ever more cracks over the years. The book looks like a catalogue whilst textually and in terms of its entire set-up it is of a different nature altogether. At the same time one could state

< None >

Henk van der Giessen
<u>Starspotting</u>

Roelof Mulder / Mevis & van Deursen

Roelof Mulder
Mevis & van Deursen

# STAR
# SPOTTING

# I could think of other, more burning issues

The project 'with a view to the future' started in September 1995.
A number of designers were asked by the Jan van Eyck Academy to come and give their vision of the future of graphic design in the Netherlands.
Each student interviewed one of the speakers. A book is to be published of the lectures and interviews. On the list of speakers are names like Wim Crouwel, Jan van Toorn, Anthon Beeke, Lies Ros, Lex Reitsma etc.; starspotting.

>> 112

to get involved in
at that time

Roelof Mulder

The word 'Future' always used to make me think of computer

generated things, something I am very far removed from.

The whole development has gone into overdrive.

All those lectures and conferences about it. All that new

media stuff. It is already getting to be like America and we

are just running to keep up? >> 110

Yes, and it is true. In America it is highly stimulated by the film industry. There you have space to grow and develop. When you do computer animation there and you do it well, before you know it, somebody is at your door offering you eighty thousand dollars a year. It is very attractive and you can make a lot of money and find a lot of work with it.

**But here you are talking about the film industry. Is that so close to design?**

Yes. For instance, that Michael Worthington, who has now gone to a multinational. He only finished his degree six months ago, made a CD-ROM about 'Call-Arts', started to work for Lorraine Wild. Then was approached by a multi-national and so disappeared in the commercial filmindustry. So-called, because it is really about all those games, CD-ROMs and everything that is happening in that field. And that is how it goes for many people who do a course in America and who say, 'I want to earn a lot of money and why not if I can'. What it has got to do with graphic design? Nothing. It goes into film, video, whatever you want to call it. You find the same thing in Hollywood when you look for instance at that film that has just come out, in which actors are animated. Soon there will be a film with Marilyn Monroe, for which somebody makes computer images based on photographs and makes a new film with it. They just reproduce them and make new films with it.

**One could take that direction but it was said at the '101' symposium that television did not kill radio. Many CD-ROMs will come out but books and magazines will still be there.**

Of course they will, but it is very interesting for graphic design and that is why time and time aga it generates discussion, because all of a sudden we can do it ourselves.

We have the Macs, the programmes and if you have a bit of time between a book and a poster you can make a CD-ROM. It takes a lot of time but we can do it ourselves at home. It is part of what is possible now and part of your field of work. But at a certain moment you make your choice and then a lot of people, especially in America, opt for the money.

**Is it not more interesting to look what is happening here in Holland. Dutch Design is highly regarded abroad and I think we look too much to the U.S.**

They are way ahead as far as computers are concerned. There has been a big re-evaluation of American graphic design in recent years. It has become much more important than what is happening here in Holland. Holland has remained classical but there they have used that whole computer business.

Now when you buy a book on graphic design, you mainly see American designers, hardly any Dutch

it is experimental, and by using computers the full potential is being used. All of a sudden Americans were able to do

raphic design, they went off their heads.
he Dutch think harder, everything is more considered.
ere, when they find out what possibilities the computer
fers their reaction is still reluctant.
**es, but Holland is running after it. Where has our**
**entity gone and how is it expressed?**
Vell, perhaps also in an aura of technology in the same way
s with American design. Maybe it is true that American
echnology is overrated, not just because of CD-ROMs but
lso because of the use of computers. They are swept up by
ne wave and now we look up to that. I notice that at the
cademy where I teach. They haven't got a clue who Jan van
born is yet they know all the American designers.
re we losing our love of print?

# do have that impression a little.
# But it is up to designers to do something about it.

can imagine that many people are not interested.
ut I am, as well as in the new media.
**Vhat happens if a client comes to you and says he needs**
**CD-ROM with a short film on the 6th and 9th tracks?**
**ou make a CD ROM with thirty others as well. You are**
**omebody with an arts background who has always**
**orked as an individual; how do you see such a role in a**
**reater whole?**
would do it without hesitation although I know nothing
bout it; why not? It would have to be an interesting
ommission, though. You can make the basic design and,
deed, a lot of people are involved, but there has to be
omebody who co-ordinates. I would definitely do it if I were
sked. I would love it, especially because I like film; it
trigues me and I miss it too. I kept that interest from my
rtist years. I did a lot with video and I think it is fantastic
hat those days have returned. I wouldn't mind getting a
ece of work like that. Only that's when the problem starts.
Vhat do you do afterwards, make another book?
**hey are not mutually exclusive, are they?**
hat is not strictly true, because you have to develop your-
elf as well and if I were to develop myself in the direction of
patial and time-based work then the two-dimensional work
ould be put aside.
**oes it have to do with the fact that you know it all**
**nyway? You design invitations, posters, stamps,**
**ooks, etc. Don't you look for other disciplines, seek**
**ew impulses?**
o, I have only been an official graphic designer for four
ears. Before that I did things in graphics but I was never
ained in it, so even now I know nothing about it.
designed stamps recently which is a good example. I did
ot know what it entailed and I picked it up over the last
hree months. You use the things you learn in a process like
hat when you go on to design a poster. In that sense it is
ood that they are all different commissions; you get the
eeling you are part of a continuous process.
**that related to the growth you were talking about?**
es. In particular in recent months I have had the feeling
am growing. I have learned a lot over the last years, every-
hing was new for me and even now the simplest things go

wrong sometimes. Sometimes I use the mistakes as well.
That is nice; you are more able to experiment that way and
that is really what I want.
**You work mainly on commission now. As a designer you**
**always have to deal with certain patterns, as an artist**
**you can ignore these to create freedom.**
But who accepts that freedom? Nobody. Yes, and then I
could also answer that question for the future. I want to
continue working to commission whilst at the same time
making sure that I do certain things by myself, to develop
and move towards a perfect balance between the
experiment, in which I can take risks, and the restraints of
commissions. Sometimes you have to be able to do strange
things without being stopped by a client. The discussion with
the client is important but your development is as well. The
experiment remains the most important thing for me.
**During the lecture somebody asked whether you had**
**become a product.**
First explain what a product is. I don't mind answering but
I find it an insulting question. I think that every designer with
a bit of a name is a product. Good designers know how to
deal with that and use it, but there aren't many of them
around in Holland.
**A product is also something recognisable.**
Yes, although sometimes I find my work is still a bit too
consistent. The things that work best deviate that little bit
from the norm. Crossing borders interests me. I am interested in exactly those works that are a bit strange and not
immediately comprehensible, which make you think: 'is this
good or isn't it?' There is a grey area, when you deviate you
are regarded as strange because people cannot place you.
I am interested in the area where you deviate a lot.
Something of which you can say later that it could have
failed but you can point out why it didn't. This happens with
editing Forum too. It deals with themes and sometimes you
end up in a fog. Things can get out of hand, meetings run
aground and then, finally, we take decisions and go for
something. And as a result a product is printed which is
completely bizarre and not a soul understands it. According
to the editors it is good but it is too extreme to be effective,
to wake people up. >> 114

# This publication had to be about your opinion...

I opted for a younger generation which meant I was to interview Roelof Mulder. To my surprise Mevis & van Deursen were not on the list. When we talk about present-day design and designers who represent a particular period it is precisely these that one cannot ignore. So I wanted them in. I find their work clear, transparent and convincing. It has continuity because they, as Mevis puts it, 'have remained close to the things, which characterise the sharpness in their work'.

But the project progressed with difficulty. Preparations got off to a slow start. There was a lack of enthusiasm and, yes, there were even conflicts in the air. 'What were your goals, what was your strategy and how did you have to prod to elicit frank answers about things you always wanted to know. Simply forget you are a designer and become a journalist.'

# Like sheep we followed our shepherds

For months we racked our brains on these questions. Things got so complicated! I continued to ask myself what good all this would do. The need for a project about Dutch design remained unclear to me. New media develop so rapidly that the inteviews will already be out-of-date by the time this publication goes to print. Is a one year old interview still topical enough? Is this what I had come to the Maastricht academy for? No! I had come here with a work plan and wanted to concentrate on that.

The future of graphic design in the Netherlands; I did not want to write a piece about that. Others could do that much better than me! I could think of other, more burning issues to get involved in at that time. I only had to look around at the kind of world we were in. Where was the concern with issues meriting the attention of designers? Here, at the Jan van Eyck started to see design >> 116

*Is that not related to the readership? The local butcher is not interested in Forum but the circle of architects, artists and designers know how to appreciate it.*

Well, we had many comments, even from our management committee, that it had too much text and not enough pictures. If you look at the result of three and a half years' work you see a product which is as a rock-solid but too extreme to have any effect. As editors we think it is good, we learn from it and use it.

*It is a magazine for architects so you expect pictures. You used mainly text. How does that work? You have to sell the idea as well.*

We have been asked as editorial staff to make those issues and we do it from our viewpoint. We take standpoints, get a lot of criticism but for the editors that is the only way to go about it.

*How did you end up in Forum?*

Designers were asked to present work. You look to see whether there is anything there for you, it has to come from two sides of course.

# It is also a question of knowing how to sell yourse a question of bullshitting well.

Take a car dealer who sells you a car that doesn't work. Every bird its song. Some people are like that. Others are asked on a wholly different basis. Of course it is not the only thing, what is important is the work, and the drive, that you are enthusiastic, that you are behind what you do, that you know what you are doing.

*The way in which you manifest yourself, express yourself, place the nuances in what you say.*

Well, I am not very subtle, I also say what I think, when I think something is bad I say it, even if the person stands next to me. I am amazed that does not happen more often, how much people can beat around the bush. That is what I hated most about being an artist. Create a discussion, I prefer a discussion.

*Can reacting to a work be a question of feeling?*

To a certain extent it is a concept and after that it becomes a question of feeling. And indeed sometimes that goes a long way. When you see a poster for instance it is a gut reaction that is being addressed. What is it saying to me, what has it to offer me? It isn't always easy to react to it; often it is about very subtle things. That is what I like about teaching. Then you have to say something about it, that way you are forced to learn it.

*Another thing. Eight designers have been chosen for this project. You are one of the younger generation; some designers have not been asked. What puts you in that position. In other words, what do you contribute to current design?*

Well, rather a lot, and it will have to become a lot more. With my experiments I help others on their way, I see it in my students. Many people appreciate my experiments and get something out of it. I think about that little book *Speed is what you need*, and how much following it got. You notice when you are being watched in the design world, that people are surprised when you make something they

haven't seen before. After the design prize things have gor quickly, after all it is a prize with a certain prestige and has helped me on my way considerably. I am still reaping th fruits of it but I want to stay small as long as possible.

*What do you mean by small?*

Well I could take somebody on to promote my products. Yo often see that kind of promotion. I don't do anything lik that, I just get commissions. I could expand if I took o somebody to promote my work. Then the orders sta flooding in, money starts flooding in and automatically become a big concern, the director of a design studio. Lik Dumbar for instance. Then you are doing your work in different way. But for the time being I like to do mad thing and experiment. I often go to Karel Martens to talk abou this as well, or Karel comes here. Sometimes it is ve important to ask someone, 'is this good or isn't it?' Workin together as well. Working with the Stedelijk went ve well. I am very satisfied with the Peiling '95 catalogue. It ha become a very intimate book. The little staples are reference to a book which Wim Crouwel made for the Stedeli Museum in the sixties. I am not happy with the cover; it ha to be ready in a hurry and that is when things go wrong I prefer making a film, which is more what the work insid is like. I prefer that process to making a picture, which more what the cover is like, an eye-catcher, a sales stun With Forum I did succeed. I made the photos on the cove myself. I have been concentrating on photography agai because I have rather got infected with Arnhem typograph I like comely photoshop work; if you master it well it is jus like scissors and tape. ■

rom the '101' symposium and the lectures at the Jan van
...ck I have got the idea that we are running after the new
...edia. Holland has a strong position as far as graphic
...sign is concerned; do we have to go chasing after the new
...edia?
...). It is not that important which medium you express
...urself in as long as you have something to say or to add.
... does not interest me whether that takes place in a book,
... invitation, on CD-ROM, on film or whatever.

> ...ou take somebody else's problem as your starting point
> ...nd you turn it into your problem; I think that is the essence
> ...f what a designer does.

...would rather like to say something with film or on
...D-ROM. I don't mind but I don't think it is interesting to
...e it as a hype, something you do because otherwise you
...e missing the boat. There are people who have always
...ade images and suddenly make a film, or somebody like
...odard, a theoretician who starts to make films; all that is
...ssible. As long as you have ideas about it; the story you
...e telling is of the essence. The moving image has been
...ry important for the development of design.
...re designers still of any relevance if we look to new
...chnology?
...). It can be expected of designers that they make things or
...ok at them with special interest. It is all about attention,
...ve, interest. If nobody loved letter types everything might
... well look the same.
...ve, interest?
...re graphic designers taken seriously at all?
...). It is not a burdened occupation. It has no status and
...ere is only a small circle who get excited about it. The
...ople who find it interesting are the designers themselves,
...body is bothered about design.
.. I think that it is undervalued. It has a much greater
...fluence on our lives in proportion to the extent to which
... is talked about. People outside design do not recognise
...e role of the designer. That role is much bigger than they
...sume, because everything is expressed visually.

> ...esigners shouldn't be concerned only with analysing a
> ...roblem and translating it, they have to be clear in their visual
> ...nguage. It is what you represent as a designer that matters.

...it related to mental attitude? When I look at your work
...ense a judgement.
.. You always think when you are working. We have
...inions about what certain things should look like. We try
... make that apparent. With every commission we get we
...n look at it anew and change it.
...). What you are saying now could mean anything; that
...rt of opinion tailors itself to the commission. I don't think

it is just reacting to design, that is too limited for the way we
work.
**But is mental attitude a guarantee to success?**
vD. You would think it is but then you have to be able to
name that attitude. We always go to the extreme in a design
and I think that has a positive influence on what happens in
design in general. It is a very open way of working. And it
shows in what we make. >> 118

# But it made me think

# Until then I had put
# designers of a certain

as a luxury problem, a product of an affluent society
'A museum catalogue is no more than a collection of
pictures and letter types' I heard Roelof Mulder say.
I strongly doubted the necessity of this project; the
future of graphic design, the little club which gets all
wound up about it. This was not a world I could identify
myself with.

Given my political experiences at the Jan van Eyck
Akademie I wanted these conversations to be personal in character. I was interested in the people
behind the design, the identity and mentality of the
designers. It did not matter to me what a person
can do, but what sort of a person he or she is.
Whether mentality has anything at all to do with
designing. Does the quality of a work matter as long
as you can package it in pretty words?
Too much design is being rationalised. So it was a

# standing on a pedestal

elief to hear, during the interviews, that design is
often made too complicated. It confirms what I had
thought initially. Design had to speak for itself more.
n talking so much about it, it becomes complex, when
t should be clear and transparent. It must have
been around March '96 that I was finally able to
make a firm appointment with Roelof Mulder. During
the interviews I was particularly interested in the
inherent contradictions: Roelof Mulder works from
a commercial standpoint and Mevis & van Deursen
come across to me as idealistic designers. With the
latter two particularly I found the conversation
clarifying and inspiring. More became clear to me in
these two interviews than in all the costly talk-filled
time at the Jan van Eyck. I was on the edge of my
chair as I listened to the recordings. Even now
essential parts keep coming back to me and I would
have liked to publish them in full. >> 120

Every time it goes just that little bit further.

M. What makes it important for others is that it is moving in a certain direction. Ideas return, work is approached in the same way and becomes recognisable that way. We concentrate hard on the development in our work. That way it can become a world on its own.

*That is not always appreciated. I am thinking of the diary you made for the KPN. How far are you either servile or, on the other hand, critical?*

vD. When people ask us, they have to realise what they are getting. We can only make something good if we have made it our own problem. Only in that way it can be interesting. With the diary it was the same thing. We thought about doing something with imagery, but how, and why. And if you are able to puzzle that out it suddenly becomes an enjoyable commission.

*You become able to bend it to your own will and you become your own problem-solver.*

M. Exactly, then you can say 'this is what we want to do with it and if we can't then we won't take it'. It does not start when we take on a commission, but it becomes interesting when we can put something of ourselves into it.

If you don't do that, you are left with solving somebody else's problems. Whereas when I want to make something of value, something that interests me, something that involves me and for which I have a view of what it should look like, that's a totally different story. That is the only attitude to have and that is, I think, what you mean by mental attitude; you have to take it extremely seriously, to such an extent that you set your own standards.

I think that what is most important is that with every commission you ask yourself why. What is the necessity? That 'Why?' is the most important question you ask yourself. The position from which you refuse a commission, is one you create yourself. You will notice that unless you take a stance you end up doing work you don't like.

You're not asked on the basis of your style but on the basis of your attitude and that attitude can only be perceived when you make it visible.

*And you are saying that attitude is your stance?*

vD. Yes, I think so. The only reason why I think we are important for the future is that we are completely local designers. You could say that we work autonomously within the field of design; we will never get attention elsewhere than in Holland.

*Not only locally. Your work is picked up on abroad.*

vD. I don't understand at all why. It has got more to do with their way of thinking, with the hunger for young Dutch designers. Maybe we represent that, so they arrive at our door, but why ours? We aren't the ambassadors of young Dutch design, are we? At the time we were starting out design took flight; it got a lot of attention. We have been lucky and the names have stuck.

M. We both worked for studio Dumbar, which has a lot of international contacts, and before you realise it your work is getting about in an international circle and you are invited.

Maybe we have been lucky, but you're never just luc[ky]. They obviously consider that what you do has to be of val[ue] and you could say that starts at the academy. When I tea[ch] at an academy it is immediately clear which people a[re] interesting. They are the ones who are going to play a ve[ry] important role in design.

vD. A very important role? You mean they will be nic[e] able to earn their keep, to get nice work.

M. But I could also ask why go to the Jan van Eyck Aka[de]mie? So as not to stop the moment you finish your init[ial] training. The people who take that extra step are the on[es] who are noticed because they are extra motivated.

*Have you ever looked for clients yourselves?*

M. Sometimes, in the beginning, and you could say tha[t] has had results. Maybe it is stupid that we no longer do [it.] I wouldn't mind doing a commercial commission to s[ee] how I would deal with it. Maybe it would be fantastica[lly]

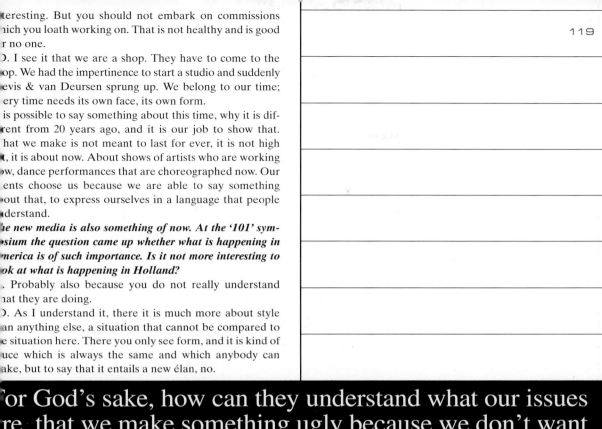

teresting. But you should not embark on commissions
which you loath working on. That is not healthy and is good
for no one.

D. I see it that we are a shop. They have to come to the
shop. We had the impertinence to start a studio and suddenly
Mevis & van Deursen sprung up. We belong to our time;
every time needs its own face, its own form.

is possible to say something about this time, why it is different from 20 years ago, and it is our job to show that.
What we make is not meant to last for ever, it is not high
art, it is about now. About shows of artists who are working
now, dance performances that are choreographed now. Our
clients choose us because we are able to say something
about that, to express ourselves in a language that people
understand.

*The new media is also something of now. At the '101' sym-*
*posium the question came up whether what is happening in*
*America is of such importance. Is it not more interesting to*
*look at what is happening in Holland?*

. Probably also because you do not really understand
what they are doing.

D. As I understand it, there it is much more about style
than anything else, a situation that cannot be compared to
the situation here. There you only see form, and it is kind of
sauce which is always the same and which anybody can
make, but to say that it entails a new élan, no.

## For God's sake, how can they understand what our issues are, that we make something ugly because we don't want it to look designed.

Yes, indeed, they believe in form.

. They make it all very complicated. Theory is very
important there; at the academies they talk about the profession in a very complicated manner, and then the students
start to complicate things too, and the work looks complicated as a result. While I think, just say what you've got to
say. Here in Holland the work is much more direct, much
simpler and clearer. I think that there is no clear public in
America. When they make a book it is only seen by
designers, a very isolated little world. We know that the
things we make are part of an ordinary world, so you have
to communicate with ordinary people. Americans do not
recognise the quality of what they do well, which is very
commercial things from an advertising point of view. It has
a harshness and directness which is inspiring for us,
something we can use. It has a clarity and power we
understand.

*The Netherlands is the most Americanised nation of*
*Europe. When I talk about new technology, I ask myself*
*whether design is of importance any more because it is all*
*about the speed of consumption.*

D. You could say that the added value of design is marginal.
It is not all as spectacular as it should be; it is just one of a
lot of things and there are only a few who see the added
value of it. That's all. And it became apparent again with
that diary. We were very happy with the result, but there
were many complaints from the KPN. It's an illusion to
think you can have an effect. At the end of the day you
have to face the facts, time and time again. You hope it will
mean something, because everything is so marginal, negli-
gible compared to the mass of information, the enormous
hodge-podge.

*But what effect are you after when you design a diary like*
*that?*

vD. The fact that it was going to be published in such
quantities was also one of the reasons for wanting to do
something with image. The visual depiction of people is so
one-sided that we thought it would be good to show new
photography from various artists. We wanted to show the
images which normally aren't shown, people in very intimate
moments, photographed in a very direct manner, and you
do not see that anywhere else apart from in the photography
we were interested in at that time.

M. Because you hope it will be picked up by people who
will see the beauty and quality of those pictures as well.

*It is picked up, but by a special public. And when you use*
*those kind of images for the KPN you know from the out-*
*set that you will be criticised.*

M. But that is what I find exciting.

vD. Of course it is in great contrast with how they present
themselves. It is after all a very different world from the
one in which everybody normally lives. What we are
showing is the super-real, the flip-side of the coin. Look, the
KPN is showing us all those energetic, >> 122

# It became clear to me that in this little

I did not feel free to do so however, and I decided to restrict myself to publishing a very condensed version and let the conversations be for what they were. But it made me think. Until then I had put designers of a certain standing on a pedestal. The ones who were given so much space and took so many liberties. In the end what becomes clear is that every designer is restricted in freedom.

Based on his interview each student designed 16 pages of the book to be published in the summer of '96. Or that was the plan. In the end this did not appear enough, and each had to add a piece of one's own. This publication had to be about your opinion; 'Treat it as if you had 30 minutes airtime on television, what would you say?' Like sheep we followed our shepherds. The lectures, talks and discussions were not very lively and nobody dared stick his neck out.

# world a particular
# attitude was
# required

And this should be the place, according to
Jan van Toorn in the de Volkskrant [Dutch newspaper],
where you had to let your hair down.
But there was an uneasy atmosphere. It became
more and more clear to me that in this little world
a particular attitude was required. The fact that it
was to be a Jan van Eyck publication weighed heavily.
The space which the whole of designing Holland
watches. Class. It all took ages, but the project had
to continue. Lies Ros pulled out.
Because of the many discussions and the repeated
criticism I lost much enthusiasm. I asked myself
where was the spontaneity, the drive, in what I wanted
to talk about? Now, in 1997, rounding off the project,
I ask myself whether it would not have been better
to use the time helping old age pensioners to cross
the road.

healthy and enthusiastic people, all cheerful families. But everybody writes letters and receives post. Post ends up on dirty doormats as well. And it was exactly those images they could not identify with.

*You wanted to make clear that everybody stinks of sweat.*

vD. Exactly, yes. And that the world of advertising is not one with which you can identify.

M. On that point we do that little something other designers do not. That you think, 'fuck it, I will do it', out of idealism, that you add something to the things that are made. Good things are made out of idealism.

vD. You have to believe in what you are doing, believe in what you want so that you can defend yourself. It is no good when what you do is totally interchangeable. You have to believe in what you do when you want it to be successful. Only that way you can be convincing. We fill the gaps; we make the books that are missing.

M. So that you can put something somewhere and think, that was still missing. Maybe the designs we make now are not picked up yet, maybe it will take another 20 years.

vD. I don't believe that at all. It has to work now. I cannot start from the premise that it will have an effect in twenty years time. Everybody knows what is happening at the moment. You have to be able to communicate it now. If it only has an effect in twenty years time you can say you have failed.

M. We can only make things because designers before us have cleared the way. What you make will have consequences for the society we live in.

vD. You could say consequences for designers. It is minuscule in proportion to the enormous mounts of shit. You hope that people can make use of the things you make, but I don't have any illusions. If people can only make use of it in twenty years then I find that a pity. It has to be of use to them now, effective now.

**But we shouldn't just think towards the public. We create a yardstick, out of our possibilities we produce what we think is good, full stop.**

Thanks to: Fonds voor de Beeldende Kunsten, Vormgeving en Bouwkunst and Evelien van Vugt.

Marion Burbulla
<u>An interview with Joseph Plateau</u>

Eliane Beyer
Wouter van Eyck
Peter Kingma
Rolf Toxopeus

→ **Joseph Plateau** is a collective of four young graphic designers situated in Amsterdam. Their strange company name comes from a Belgian scientist from the 19th century, who created the first basic prototypes for film-projectors. However, his main dedication in life was research into different functions of the eye.

Unfortunately during one of his investigations he looked at the sun for too long and went blind. But this did not stop him from continuing his studies and writing a book on the amazing effect of the after image in the eye.

The collective was so impressed by this person that they decided to name their company after him. Eliane Beyer, Wouter van Eyck, Peter Kingma and Rolf Toxopeus are the four people behind this name.

**Joseph Plateau** were recently invited to the Jan van Eyck Akademie as representatives of young Dutch graphic designers. The following interview should give a brief overview of their practical work and theoretical approaches in the field of graphic design practice.

An Interview with

# Joseph Plateau

MARION **What is the history of Joseph Plateau?**

ROLF We met each other at the Rietveld Academy in Amsterdam at evening classes. We were among a group of 12 students and gradually realised that there was some affinity in our work. Each of us was enthusiastic about what the others made and felt inspired by the work of the other three. Alongside that an ordinary friendship started to develop. These were the two basic ingredients that more or less started the collective the way it is today.

MARION **Exactly when was that?**

ROLF We started the academy in 1984/85 and the collective was formed in 1989. About half way through 1987 Wouter was involved with a commission outside school for the 'Desmet Film Theater', and was asked to design a brochure for them. He wanted to do it together with us. That was one of the first things we did together. Not long after that the school approached us as a group and asked us to work for one or two initiatives they were taking on as an institute.

PETER Each of us had already done something else before. Rolf and I were giving drawing lessons to high-school students, Wouter had not finished his studies, Eliane was studying technical design. When I was studying with the others I was thinking quite a lot about what I would like to do after school. I had faced the problem before that

# I didn't want to be a teacher!

So by talking about these things, we liked the idea of forming a group. We didn't know how it would finally work but the initial idea was to form a group that would continue after school.

ROLF Some of the work we showed at the graduation show was Joseph Plateau work and some of it was under our own individual names.

WOUTER Well, one could say that what we did at school was totally impractical. You could even say that we were not really busy with graphic design in a way you should practice it after school. We experienced and learned things about graphic design from a much broader perspective. It was interesting to continue this common sense approach which is different from the practical and professional sense of graphic design. In this way we could retain strong attitudes.

MARION How would you define the difference between these two senses?

WOUTER It was more about developing your own personality in combination with visual images.

There was not much emphasis on typography and we learned very little about the production side.

MARION But don't you think that it is more important that you have time to develop your own personality because all the technical things can be learnt quite quickly?

WOUTER Yes, after all we strongly agreed very much with this education.

*And for us it was important to continue with this kind of education in a more professional way.*

MARION Why did you choose as four people to work together under one name?

ROLF We wanted to present ourselves as one person and not as a group of four. That was the initial idea and it seemed funny to us. The fifth person is what you are left with at the end. Add it all up.

MARION Does this idea still work?

ROLF Today is quite a different story. The idea of working together was also inspired by the idea that many people fall straight into a black hole after finishing college. All of a sudden the commissions and the guidance of the teachers are not there anymore and you miss the support from them as well as from your fellow students. In order to bridge that gap we thought it would be a good idea to stay together with a group of people with whom you feel you have something in common.

MARION And you never wanted to work for anyone else?

ROLF No, I think that one of the things we had in common was that none of the four fancied a job under some supervision, a superior designer.

MARION **What is the situation today?**

ROLF It's very much in progress. Since we've started we've been adapting ourselves to the changes within and outside. Right now we are looking at possible ways to give more room to the individual idea and at the same time create some sort of structure that enables us to get as much as possible out of the fact that we are together four people and not just working on our own in a studio in town.

PETER In practice this means that if we get an exceptionaly complicated, new or interesting assignment we work on it together. A lot of the daily things that we also need to do for a living, we try to do it as individually as possible. There are two reasons for this: one is that we found out that collaborating takes a lot of effort and energy. But most of those things are not worth the effort. We feel that it is better and easier to do them on our own.

*Wouter and I are now working together on something*
## *that is a bit commercial for us.*

It is for factory producing. We have to design four mailings and we feel that the work we are doing is very close to the work which a normal advertising studio does. We have to maintain a careful balance between being very commercial on the one hand and on the other hand finding a limit in which you can still feel that you are delivering some quality which is not strictly commercial.

MARION Is that sometimes contradictory?

PETER Not necessarily. And that is why we are doing it. But the funny thing is that you feel all the time that you are selling something.

MARION Aren't you always selling?

PETER No, not like that, not so bluntly.

MARION What about selling cultural posters?

PETER There is more to them. You can have more idealistic ideas and you can identify more with them.

## It is a very strange thing with commercial work. There you use the ideology as an extra, but the real target is selling.

### In cultural work it is the other way round.

The ideology is the message you try to bring across and you hope that it sells.

But even this is not strictly true because I think that commercial companies are also interested in new ideas like, for example, how to think about chairs or whatever. It is not simply that they are only concerned with selling but it is also the case that they are interested in how they can go into the future as a company, how they could develop themselves, and enable themselves to continue.

MARION Is working with commercial briefs a challenge?

WOUTER Yes, if it turns out that what we think is interesting for the future is also interesting for the client, then I think it is a good combination. And if the job is working out in a way that we like then I am very proud of it.

PETER I find the nicest people to work for are the people who trust you, so that you do not have to prove at every stage of the process that things are going to work out. That makes it easy to get along with each other, but if you have this mistrust or if the process gets slowed down too much by things like having to make presentations all the time, then that is something that I don't really like.

I also mentioned the commerciality before because that is something which we are not really used to, it is something new. We haven't sold chairs before. The most commercial thing we did before was to make an annual report for a bigger company.

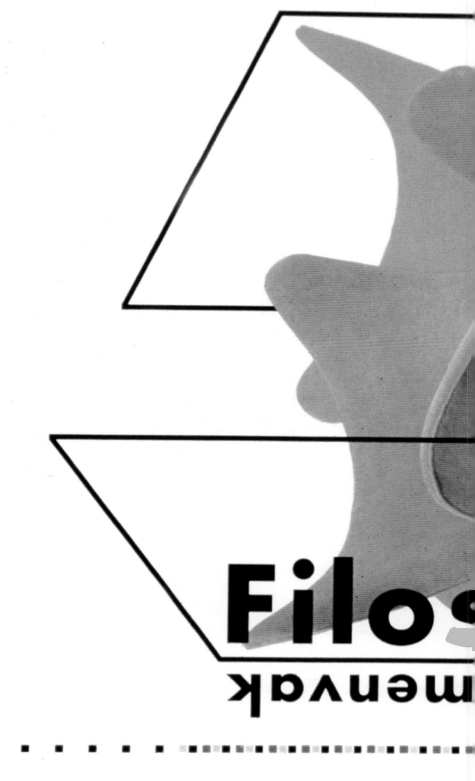

Filos

ofie

MARION Is it true that in Holland people make a strong distinction between cultural and commercial clients?

PETER A lot of companies, or rather; institutions, that we work for, are funded by the government, like the Design Institute, for example. Though they are trying to get their own commercial support and sponsorships etc.. And still most of the clients we are working for are funded one way or another.

MARION What does that mean for you?

ROLF It is probably an advantage because it makes people who commission us less tense about the success of the whole thing. They have some kind of financial guarantee anyway. So when you do commercial work the success of the campaign you are working on, or the thing you make, becomes a lot more important because if you don't get the message across, or if you don't influence people in their choices then the product might not sell and the firm might go bankrupt!

If you think about making a commercial campaign do you see that as the work of a graphic designer?

MARION Yes, I think so, because a graphic designer for me is a visual communicator and also a cultural commentator. We always influence people and we always comment on what is around at the moment.

MARION How would you define this term 'Dutch Designer'? Do you feel as though you are one of them?

PETER When I tried to work in another country, I found out that the thing that I thought was graphic design didn't exist over there. That was in Israel, but it could have been anywhere. Everybody who is working out there, is in one way or another doing commercial things for a living.

I showed them the books I made on the ampersand and they looked at me with glancing eyes and said 'You made a book about this one thing?'

*I think this is very Dutch. People like us who specialise in doing things that make no sense,*

## *so far from graphic capitalism!*

It was shocking for me. I thought I had a very international profession.

MARION Do you think Holland is a graphic design paradise ?

↑ ↑ ↑ ↑

ROLF I think abroad design is more about style. So if you ask whether it is a graphic design paradise here it just depends on what sort of graphic design you are talking about. If you are talking about a graphic designer who is looking for a way to express his own ideas then I think Holland is probably one of the better places to work because it is more about your own personal idea.

WOUTER We look for ideas and mentalities and take those as ingredients and as a starting point to make designs. It is a tradition in a certain area of Dutch design.

PETER I think the big difference is that here is a large non-commercial circuit in which there is a lot of money for designers and a lot of extra attention and effort to

PETER *Maybe it is a*

# Designer's holiday
## *instead of a paradise!*

There is a lot of style here too and there are a lot of people trying to use their certain formulas.

# give shape even to *a small fart!*

This is the holiday I was thinking of. But the other things are exactly the same as in other countries. Some people deal more with the ingredients, others deal more with the shape of the cake, and that is the same everywhere. I don't think that this is specifically Dutch. That is a design reserve here, and that area that is protected.

The values that come out of this area tend to deal more with the meaning of graphic design. It is more like what art is doing. Art is constantly introspecting and that is what is also happening in graphic design.

ROLF But if that doesn't happen you fall back on successful formulas. And if you do so then you are talking about styling.

↓ ↓ ↓ ↓

**De Boom van van Jules Verne**
EINDE VAN HET MILLENNIUM TIJDPERK DER TWEE WERELDEN

anne
5·1·93

roos
21·8·93

mart
21·10·93

**Lichaam en Taal**

**0**

**Toekomstvisies**

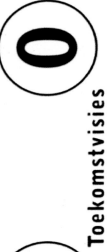

**2**

hniek

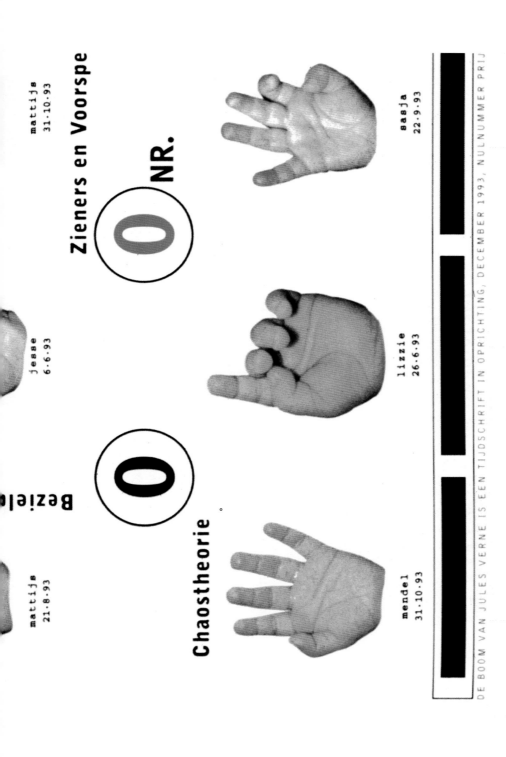

mattijs
31·10·93

# Zieners en Voorspe

0 NR.

sasja
22·9·93

jesse
6·6·93

0

lizzie
26·6·93

# Bezielo

mattijs
21·8·93

# Chaostheorie

mendel
31·10·93

DE BOOM VAN JULES VERNE IS EEN TIJDSCHRIFT IN OPRICHTING, DECEMBER 1993, NULNUMMER PRIJ

MARION How important you think style is in your work?

# Style is not important!

PETER Our idea about the look comes from the ingredients, mostly. I think that is a better way of looking at style then the seasons of styles. It should come naturally from the combination of the assignment and your personal qualities.

MARION But you can't deny that you have a certain style.

PETER There is something very fixed in this term. I don't think that style is as important as most people think it is.

ROLF I agree. When there is something that you can copy easily that is the style that has become too fashionable and it becomes a prison.

# The only unique thing you have is your own personality

and the fact that it gets crossed with some sort of uniqueness in the assignment you get. As long as you try to stick as close as possible to these two factors of uniqueness then it can't get repetitious because the assignment will be different every time and you will probably be different because you have lived for another few months.

MARION In this context what do you think about the article in 'Eye' magazine in which Joseph Plateau was described as Vorreiter of the 'New Sobriety' in Dutch graphic design. This article dealt a lot with style.

ROLF Well, I recognised a lot of what the author was saying but on the other hand I feel that he went too far in trying to prove a point that he had already made before the actual interview. He uses the term Calvinistic and I felt that far as the design of Joseph Plateau was concerned, it was just not the right way of describing it. He tried to prove his point by comparing us to people who, in his eyes, dared to go along with a more experimental way of designing.

I also feel that experimenting is an essential ingredient in your own develop-

WOUTER ment and in your own process, therefore I think in that sense I don't feel as much like being a member of the 'new sobriety' as we were portrayed, but I do recognise a certain need for basic design. So whatever I do or decide or choose, I try to make a connection with its origins.

WOUTER I think the statement is too much about style. The accent of the article is about how things look and the ideas behind it are not important.

MARION While you were at the Jan van Eyck Akademie you said that graphic designers should take responsibility for what they are doing. How do you apply that in your own work?

WOUTER I think responsibility is about being part of a process and not only about providing a service. If you take the chair manufacturer, for example, he tells you what he wants you to do and then you should ask yourself whether you can do that or not. If you can't be responsible for the action yourself then it might be better not to do such a commission.

# You always have to be responsible for yourself first.

I don't think you can fool yourself. If you haven't found your own responsibility then you will be confronted with it sooner or later. That is my experience.

MARION Do you think graphic design has a duty or a task?

WOUTER It is not just about graphic design. It is about everything. It is not specific for graphic design.

MARION What will be the future role of graphic designers, especially with the influence of new media?

PETER It seems as if there is a new specialism for which one has to train oneself and if you don't do that then you are out. You have to broaden yourself and make your way into it. The funny thing is that if you are referring to interactive design which I think is a nice area and involves a lot of other media like movement and sound, it is really a different story from what we were trained in. In the interactive area you also have to make models of how people react and it is like a small new science like ergonomics. I don't know if

we will move into this area. If we do that then we will have to put a lot of effort into it.

MARION Are you interested in making that step?

PETER Yes, I am curious. But there is no economic necessity for us to do it. It is more curiosity.

MARION Do you think that therefore the role of the graphic designer has changed or is going to change?

PETER I think it is definitely changing. One can see it in two ways. You could say: the field of graphic design is becoming bigger because of the new media but you could also see it as new specialisation, which means that the role of the graphic design becomes very specific. In both cases there will be a big change. We have to learn a lot more.

WOUTER Isn't it more about what you think will happen? Or what you want to happen.

PETER What I want to happen? To be lying in my bed and everything comes into my head while I am sleeping and the next morning I wake up and I can do all these things!

WOUTER *More holiday than you have already? More Dutchness?*

## You could die holy!

I think the question is whether there is a division or if there is a specialisation. If everybody believes in that then it maybe will happen that we will have all kinds of specialists. But then there will be a need for more exchange and more collaboration between graphic designers and people who are busy with new technology. In that way things might come together and also create new things. The possibilities for the graphic designer are changing now. I personally think that it is not very interesting to say that the field we have now will close up but I think it is interesting and also difficult to broaden out in the professional field and to stay close to the basic ingredients again. To me that sounds more attractive than that everything should stay apart in different disciplines.

**PETER** *The strange thing with all this computer technology is that* **you become more and more a producer of messages.**

You don't need to print out on paper and there are almost no costs if you do everything yourself and you can put it on the net and people from all over the world can read it. But at the same time you can do more and more yourself. You need fewer and fewer people to do this. You can be totally self supporting if you have a computer and a scanner.

MARION Then you would need a designer to organise all this information. On the net there is a vast amount of information and after a while you don't know anymore where you are and where to search for useful information and what to select. Don't you think the designer is shifting towards becoming an information designer?

PETER Yes, that is something that we will need or what we already need. If you are going to design a site with a lot of information and a lot of pages which are-updated regularly then you have to be very clever in an editorial sense.

WOUTER I believe there will be a connection between printed work and the web. If we design things for paper then they could be related to websites or the other way round. Whether you like it or not in the near future you will deal with both media. There is also a great need for communication about it. You have to work together to bring out this information in two directions. In this way you will learn and be confronted with the advantages of the other media.
You will be able to choose between presenting your information on the net or on a floppy or a CD-ROM or on paper. It is just another layer. There will be a kind of mixture.
But a lot of information will not be printed anymore. A lot of information will only be on the net and even information which is now not available will be available in future because this is a new possibility.

I think the graphic designer, if he is able to use the technology, should choose which medium

WOUTER would be appropriate for certain commissions. Therefore he has to talk to the commissioner about what the best solution or the best medium would be.

*Today there is still a gap between new media and printed matter but*

## I think soon it will be the same as deciding between a brochure or a poster.

PETER There is definitely no end of print in sight. It is just that a lot of things will not be printed anymore. It will be a shift and it will also become more expensive and luxurious to print.

Will Joseph Plateau work in the field of new media in the near future?

MARION At the moment it is still theoretical.

WOUTER I think in the future we will work in that area.

ROLF I don't think so.

PETER the end...

The interview was held by Marion Burbulla.

Cesare Davolio
<u>Futuro present</u>

Because I am not Dutch or a designer, to take a view to the future (of design) first meant to look at a past I knew nothing about and to document a present which I had moved through only as an observer. I wanted to document my personal experience of Dutch design as I encountered it daily through the city of Amsterdam, the place where I live. My ignorance of the graphic design scene forced me to engage with Amsterdam's chaotically plastered surface, with its complex visual imageries and congested texture. As an Italian artist I wanted to know what were the social conditions that created such fertile ground for the arts and design.

Alongside this not only visual, but tactile experience of design in the street, I wanted to satisfy my curiosity with regards to the attention it is given in the Netherlands. How had socialism impacted its design? Is there a Dutch aesthetic when it comes to visualizing information? I wanted to see and not just to

idtf.ro present

Amsterdam'daki Anadolu
Anatolië in Amsterdam

**100k**, confronting my

own desires and expectations about design as an

important element in the construction of culture.

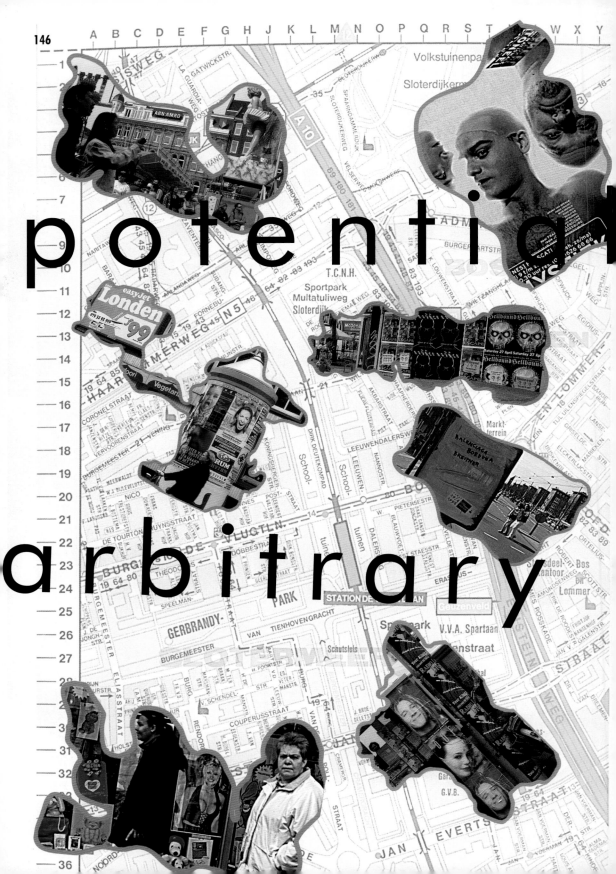

potential

arbitrary

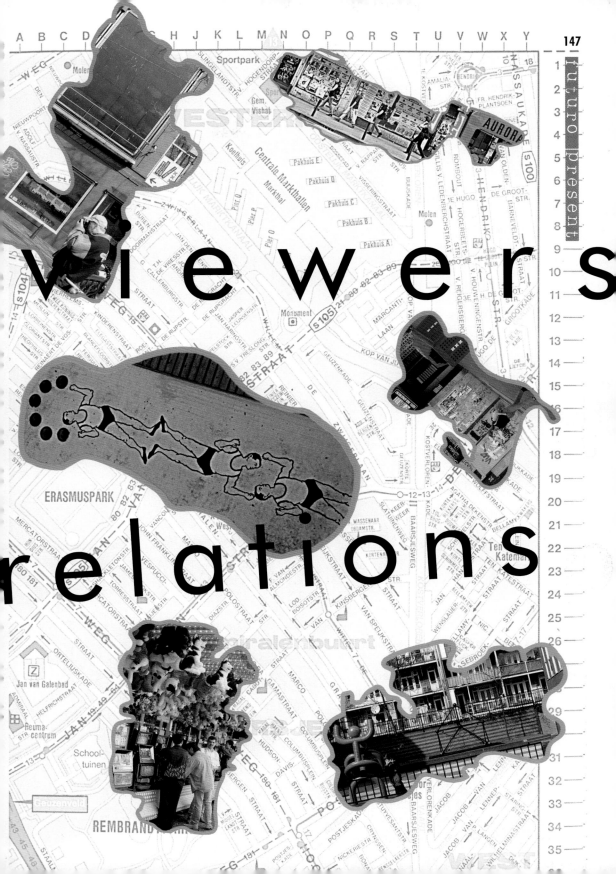

viewers

relations

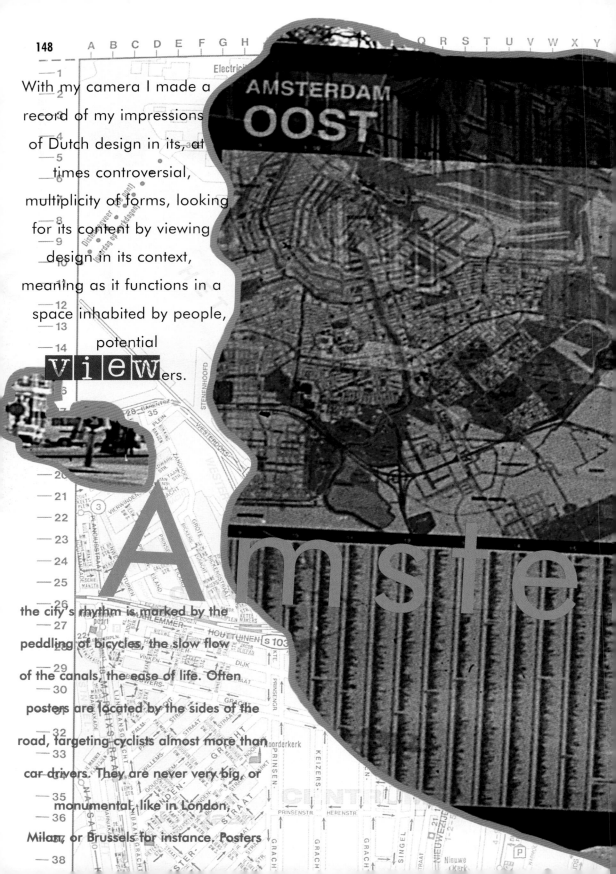

With my camera I made a
record of my impressions
of Dutch design in its, at
times controversial,
multiplicity of forms, looking
for its content by viewing
design in its context,
meaning as it functions in a
space inhabited by people,
potential **viewers.**

the city's rhythm is marked by the
peddling of bicycles, the slow flow
of the canals, the ease of life. Often
posters are located by the sides of the
road, targeting cyclists almost more than
car drivers. They are never very big, or
monumental, like in London,
Milan, or Brussels for instance. Posters

and advertisement are quite modest in scale forcing an intimacy with cyclists who reads passing by often must stop to small details of information. It is perhaps an old remainder, in accordance with Calvinist tradition of closely studying the Scriptures. A streak of strictness runs through Dutch aesthetic, exemplified by Mondrian, whom not by chance looked like a severe school master. His paintings are a deliberate and rational strive towards abstraction, where it is all pure, a desire to embrace universally forms clear and simple

Historically, a long-standing tradition of socialist government has created a strong economy, a welfare state enviably efficient compared to many countries. It has been said the standard of quality of much post-war design originated by the unique relationship namely between designers and commissioners, companies and the industries, not to mention the close ties between graphic designers, and artisans, artists, that

**around** 1900 started to work very closely with the industries. Being a relatively small country, designers would be introduced to companies by other designers. In this free climate the industries felt a sense of responsibility towards the social condition of its workers. It was an interest of the whole of society, to improve on housing, education, and architecture, but also art and graphic design. Amsterdam is a beautiful example of this effort, based on improving working performances but also human values. After WW2 state companies like PTT (Postal service), Dutch Railways, and many others, increasingly looked at design, not only for its commercial values but above all for its quality. Independent trades, industries, and government agencies, joined forces to make sure that everything from train stations to post offices and road signs should be conceived and built, not just according to function but with an aesthetic sense of harmony and order. In **the** past this was

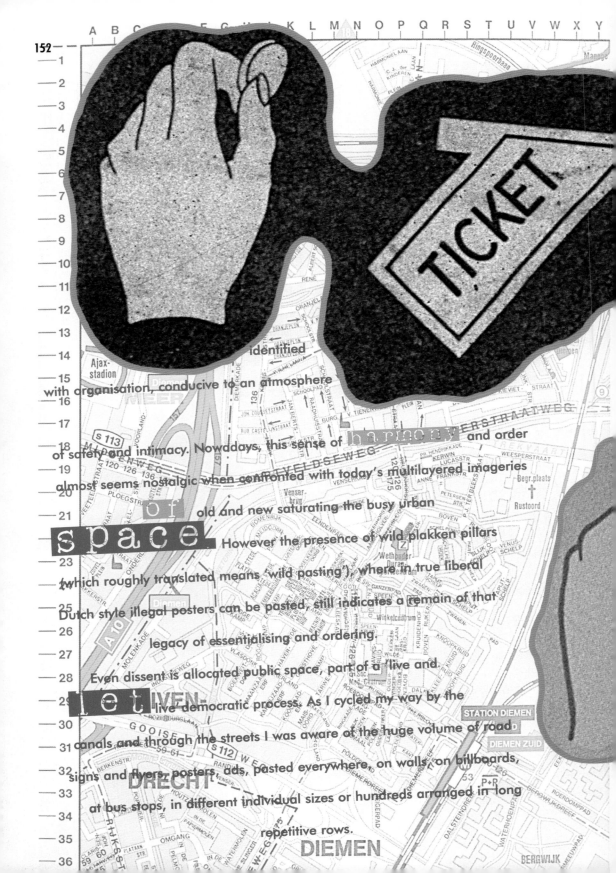

identified with organisation, conducive to an atmosphere of safety and intimacy. Nowadays, this sense of harmony and order almost seems nostalgic when confronted with today's multilayered imageries of old and new saturating the busy urban space. However the presence of wild plakken pillars (which roughly translated means 'wild pasting'), where in true liberal Dutch style illegal posters can be pasted, still indicates a remain of that legacy of essentialising and ordering.

Even dissent is allocated public space, part of a 'live and let live' democratic process. As I cycled my way by the canals and through the streets I was aware of the huge volume of road signs and flyers, posters, ads, pasted everywhere, on walls, on billboards, at bus stops, in different individual sizes or hundreds arranged in long repetitive rows.

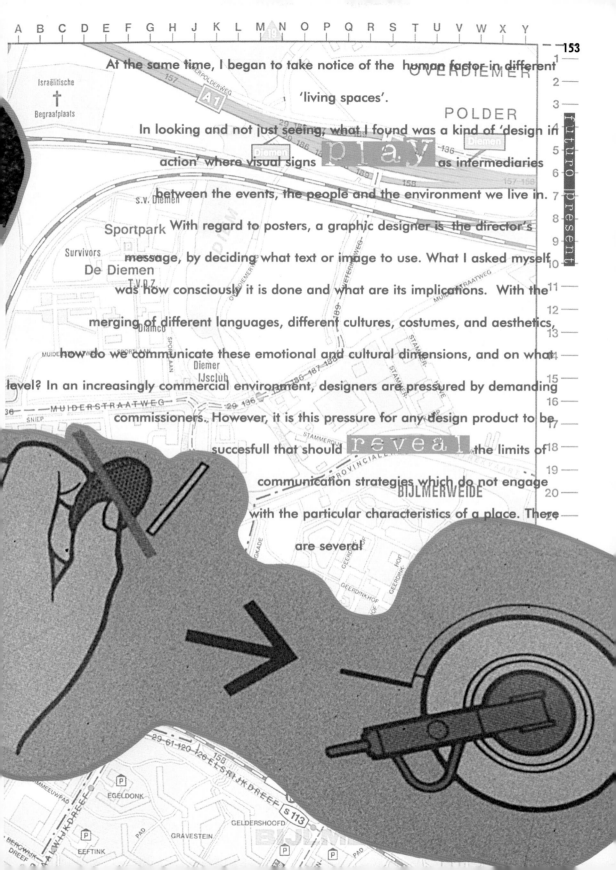

At the same time, I began to take notice of the human factor in different 'living spaces'.

In looking and not just seeing, what I found was a kind of 'design in action' where visual signs **play** as intermediaries between the events, the people and the environment we live in. With regard to posters, a graphic designer is the director's message, by deciding what text or image to use. What I asked myself was how consciously it is done and what are its implications. With the merging of different languages, different cultures, costumes, and aesthetics, how do we communicate these emotional and cultural dimensions, and on what level? In an increasingly commercial environment, designers are pressured by demanding commissioners. However, it is this pressure for any design product to be succesfull that should **reveal** the limits of communication strategies which do not engage with the particular characteristics of a place. There are several

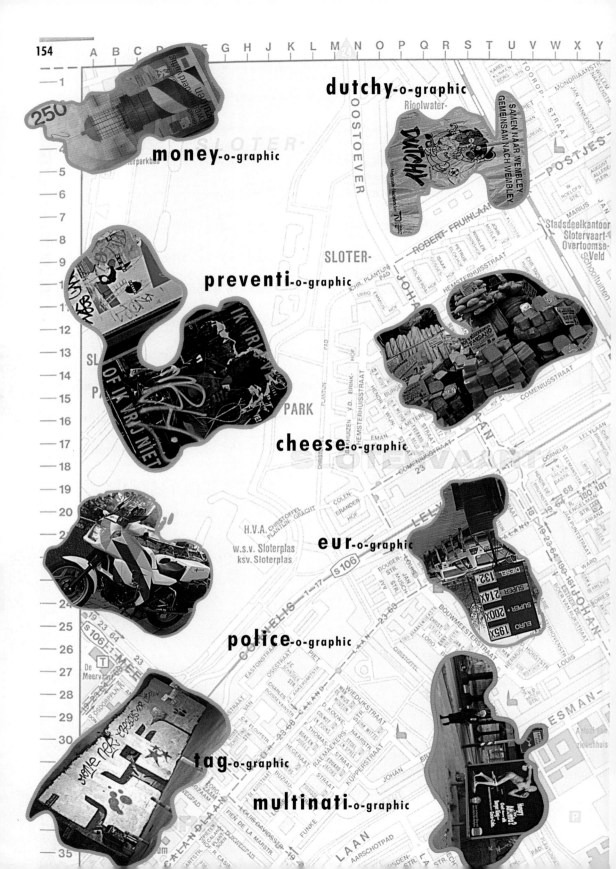

**dutchy**-o-graphic

**money**-o-graphic

**preventi**-o-graphic

**cheese**-o-graphic

**eur**-o-graphic

**police**-o-graphic

**tag**-o-graphic

**multinati**-o-graphic

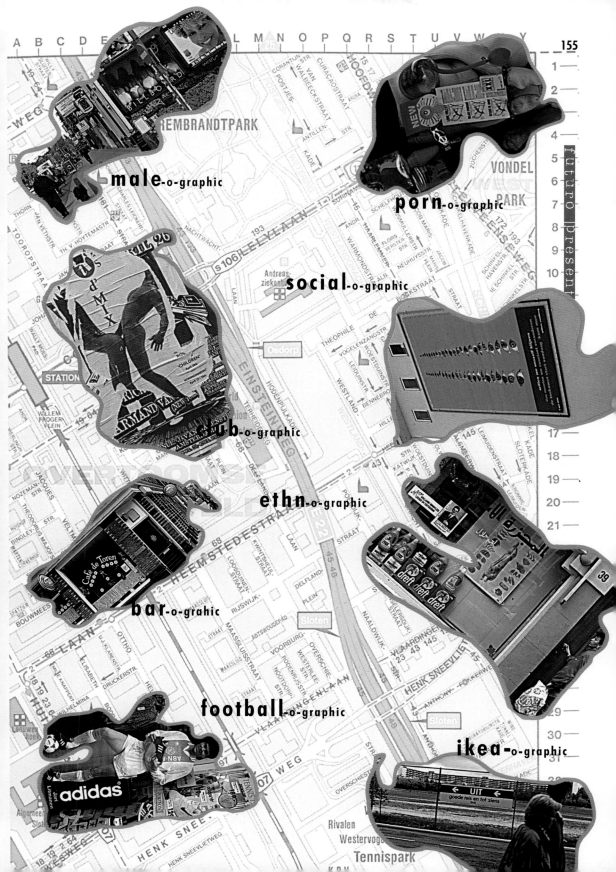

**male**-o-graphic

**porn**-o-graphic

**social**-o-graphic

**club**-o-graphic

**ethn**-o-graphic

**bar**-o-grahic

**football**-o-graphic

**ikea**-o-graphic

futuro present

influences

on design that go far beyond a studio practice; this framework constitutes a physical context consciously or unconsciously playing an important role in reading the intended message of images. At street level, my impression of Dutch design was, as far from its presentation abroad. Designers have little control over their products as theatre, museums and exhibition posters are plastered in direct juxtaposition to announcements of Suriname disco parties, rock concerts tours, and hand made signs pleading for help to find lost pets. Th

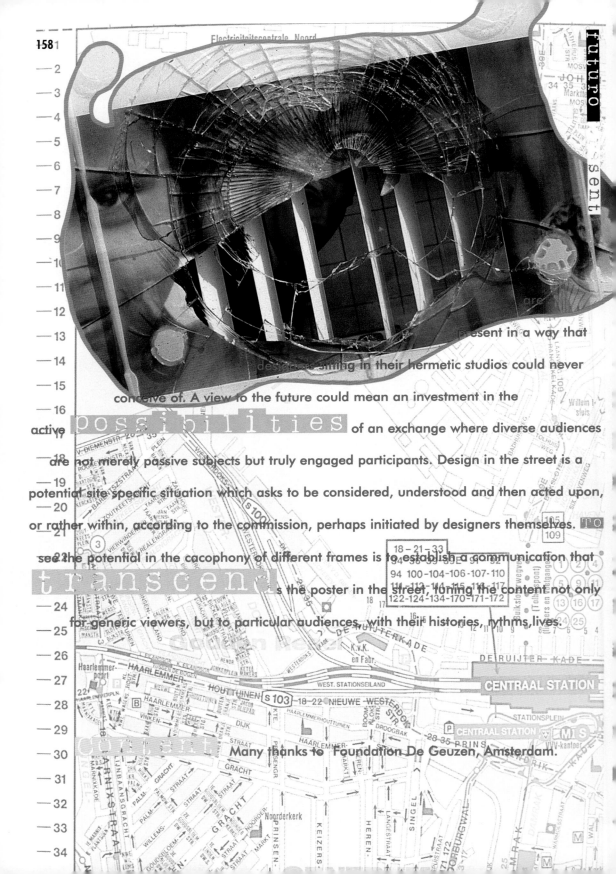

present in a way that designers sitting in their hermetic studios could never conceive of. A view to the future could mean an investment in the active possibilities of an exchange where diverse audiences are not merely passive subjects but truly engaged participants. Design in the street is a potential site specific situation which asks to be considered, understood and then acted upon, or rather within, according to the commission, perhaps initiated by designers themselves. To see the potential in the cacophony of different frames is to establish a communication that transcends the poster in the street, tuning the content not only for generic viewers, but to particular audiences, with their histories, rythms, lives.

Many thanks to Foundation De Geuzen, Amsterdam.

Colophon

Editor
Paul Hefting

Translation
[sic] Translations (Niels Biersteker, Job van Bennekom, Henk van der Giessen)

Editing
[sic] Translations
Renée Turner (Cesare Davolio)

Proof reading
Jean Fisher

Design (cover and preface)
Karel Martens

Photography (cover)
Daniël van der Velden

Co-ordination
Paul Domela Nieuwenhuis

Technical Support
Jo Frenken

Printing
Drukkerij Lecturis bv, Eindhoven

Binding
Mathieu Geertsen

Publishers
Department of Design, Jan van Eyck Akademie /
De Balie, Amsterdam

Distribution
The Netherlands: De Balie, Amsterdam
Other countries; Idea Books, Amsterdam